Praise

EVERYDA

T0008562

"*Everyday MAGIC* isn't the type of book you read once, twice, or even thrice. You'll end up highlighting your favorite parts so you can refer back to them...which is exactly what we did. Mattie will inspire you, encourage you, and remind you that you're not alone on your good days and your bad days."

—Clea Shearer and Joanna Teplin,
co-founders of *The Home Edit*

"*Everyday MAGIC* is a refreshing dose of wisdom that reminds us that we don't have to be superwoman to live full, nourishing, and powerful lives of our own design. Mattie gives women the blueprint to redefine success unapologetically by embracing her own God-given MAGIC."

—Patrice C. Washington, award-winning
host of the *Redefining Wealth* podcast

"If you're faking the enjoyment of your day-to-day life, lacking motivation, or unsure of what to do next, *Everyday MAGIC* is for you. Mattie's gift is evident through her inspiring stories and tactical strategies to help you live what you love without doing it all. If you know it's time to quiet the noise of the world and come back to your own heartbeat, this book is for you."

—Jenna Kutcher, podcaster and author of
How Are You, Really?

"Mattie curates her life in a way that allows her to make living with only what she enjoys AND alongside her family. I am consistently inspired by her and *Everyday MAGIC* is no different! *Everyday MAGIC* is goals—the kind that are outlined, attainable, and can be completely tailored to each of us. I'm so grateful to Mattie for sharing her framework on living well."

—Codie Oliver, CEO of Black Love, Inc. and
co-director of the docuseries *Black Love*

"Being a woman can be hard, and being a mom can be even harder. Today, our lives look different from those of our mothers and the women we admire that came before us. What Mattie has wonderfully outlined in this essential read is how to capture what we all innately possess, even though we may have lost it or have yet to discover it—our MAGIC."   —Tonya Rapley, author and CEO of *My Fab Finance*

EVERYDAY MAGIC

The Joy of Not Being Everything
and Still Being
MORE THAN ENOUGH

MATTIE JAMES

WORTHY
PUBLISHING

New York • Nashville

Worthy
Hachette Book Group
1290 Avenue of the Americas, New York, NY 10104
worthypublishing.com
twitter.com/worthypub

Originally published in hardcover August 2022.

First Trade Paperback Edition: August 2023

Worthy is a division of Hachette Book Group, Inc. The Worthy name and logo are trademarks of Hachette Book Group, Inc.

The publisher is not responsible for websites (or their content) that are not owned by the publisher.

The Hachette Speakers Bureau provides a wide range of authors for speaking events. To find out more, go to hachettespeakersbureau.com or email HachetteSpeakers@hbgusa.com.

Print book interior design by Bart Dawson.

Library of Congress Cataloging-in-Publication Data
Names: James, Mattie, author.
Title: Everyday magic : the joy of not being everything and still being
    more than enough / Mattie James.
Description: First Edition. | New York, NY : Worthy, 2022.
Identifiers: LCCN 2022004462 | ISBN 9781546002222 (hardcover) | ISBN
    9781546002246 (ebook)
Subjects: LCSH: Self-actualization (Psychology) | Self-realization.
Classification: LCC BF637.S4 J354 2022 | DDC 158—dc23/eng/20220330
LC record available at https://lccn.loc.gov/2022004462

ISBNs: 978-1-5460-0222-2 (hardcover); 978-1-5460-0223-9 (trade paperback);
    978-1-5460-0224-6 (ebook)

Printed in the United States of America

LSC-C

Printing 1, 2023

For Christopher, my love
and the most MAGIC person in my life.

CONTENTS

INTRODUCTION

Allow Me to Introduce Myself

A few years ago, a friend of mine who worked at a law firm was reading my blog when a coworker asked her what she was reading.

"My friend Mattie has a blog where she shares her favorite style and beauty products. You should check her out."

"Okay, I will. What's her website?"

Back then, I had a blog called *Mattieologie* where I posted outfits and beauty product reviews for readers. My friend gave her my site and social media info and the coworker followed up the next day at their office.

"So, I checked out your little friend and I mean, I don't get it.

She's just a regular Black girl." My friend was shocked at her coworker's response. Why wouldn't being a regular Black woman be enough to talk about clothes and makeup? This friend and her coworker were both Black women like me. Everything ain't for everybody, so it's totally fine that my blog wasn't for her, but in hindsight, her response revealed that she had missed the point.

That *was* the point: I am a regular, everyday Black girl. I'm not everything to everybody, and I'm fine with that. But I'm an everyday Black girl who works really hard to make my life MAGIC. That is more than enough.

We'll get back to this story in a moment, but before we go any further, allow me to introduce myself. I'm Mattie, a wife and mom based in Atlanta. Chris and I have been married for twelve years and have three amazing kids—Maizah, Caliana, and Christian. In 2009, I had the honor of winning Miss Liberia USA and started blogging soon after. Today, I'm the influencer and entrepreneur behind The Mattie James Company and BOSSFLUENCE. I create content online for my website, MattieJames.com, and @themattiejames across social media while influencing my followers to buy products I create or from brand partners like Amazon, Gerber, T.J.Maxx, and Clinique. I also teach influencers how to pitch brands and create content at a full-time level. For the last seven years, I've worked for myself as an influencer, which has helped me learn much about myself, the women I create content for, and the products we use every day. At The Mattie James Company, our mission is to create content, products, and experiences that encourage women to thrive in their everyday lives and take the mysticism out of living well.

Between you and me, I started blogging because I really enjoy my everyday life and I want other women to enjoy theirs too. I felt this way over a decade ago, when only my mom and a couple of people from my high school read my blog and I was working retail. And now, just like then, every day is not perfect—far from it. I don't cross all the items off my to-do list, I disappoint people who expect more from me, work overwhelms me because I didn't say no, the house is sometimes messier than I'd like to admit, and I order takeout when I originally intended to cook. But at the end of the day, I still love myself and my life even when I'm not everything to everyone because I understand that I'm more than enough.

Honestly, it's a little deeper than just a sunny disposition, and from what I can remember, I've always been this way.

Growing up with immigrant parents from Liberia, my mom and dad always reminded my sister and me how fortunate we were to have the life we did, and they were right. We knew so many friends and relatives who had endured unfortunate circumstances due to the Liberian civil war in the late '80s and early '90s. I watched as my very hardworking parents willingly helped their parents, siblings, and close friends get back on their feet in a variety of ways even during their own humble beginnings. When my parents moved to the US in 1980 after my dad received a scholarship to The Ohio State University, they lived in an efficiency apartment that was about 500 square feet in size. My mom always did her best to make our house a home, whether we lived in a one-bedroom apartment or a five-bedroom home while she worked her retail gig. Whether she made lunch for my dad to take to work or hosted a holiday party, she always gave 100 percent. She was honest about when she was tired; she'd rest and then start again where she left off. My dad is also a hard worker—an incredibly brilliant man who has always put forth an effort to give us what he believed to be the best. He always affirmed me and my sister by telling us we could do anything as long as we were willing to work for it, and he set very high expectations for us. By no means were my parents perfect, but they certainly did their best with purpose. And through it all, my parents enjoyed their lives. They would take us on vacations, make birthdays and holidays a big deal, have parties where they would celebrate with their loved ones, and consistently gave to others without complaint or resentment. If I'm being honest, I learned that every day could be MAGIC because of their example. By 2010—thirty years after they moved to this country—they lived in a house seven times the size of their efficiency on the campus of The Ohio State University. But their lives were MAGIC not because of things, but because of their perspective.

While we moved from Huntsville, Alabama (where I was born), to Saudi Arabia (where I attended preschool), when I was a kid, the bulk of my childhood was spent between Atlanta (elementary school), Philadelphia (middle school), and Pittsburgh (high school and college).

As a kid, I always believed that I could succeed at whatever I decided to try. Becoming an honor roll student, making the cheerleading squad, and serving as an editor for my school newspaper—these are all things I achieved growing up. My disciplinarian father wanted me to make straight As and I wanted to please him. The mistake I used to make was that I believed if I wanted to achieve something that mattered to me, it should be easy or come naturally to me, and that mindset resulted in my getting Bs and Cs instead. I believed that if I daydreamed about and envisioned being good at playing the violin, I would be entitled to playing it well. I was average at best and lessons were a waste of my time and my parents' money. I thought that because I was nice and friendly with the girls who played basketball, I would make the team. Turns out that being nice is not a prerequisite for developing your basketball skills, or any skill for that matter. Being kind matters, but it is not a substitute for doing the work.

In my twenties, I went to a satellite campus of Penn State until my junior year. After transferring once to Robert Morris University to be closer to home after I realized that college wasn't the walk in the park that high school was, I dropped out of school and moved to New York City to fulfill my dream of being a pop star. I soon learned that a consistent work ethic wasn't expected just in school; it was necessary in real life as well.

In hindsight, my experience in NYC taught me about hustle. During the day, I was a temp for the merchandising director at the Macy's corporate office; and at night, I was an assistant to my friend Forrest, who was a party promoter. Those were two jobs that required me to be intentional, even though they were temporary. My boss at Macy's was very demanding, requiring me to handle small odd jobs around the clock. And even though getting into parties for free was quite the perk at my other gig in the evenings, I still had to put fires out and make sure the party went as planned. At twenty-two, it was quite the learning curve for me. I was operating on a schedule where I had to be everything to my two bosses, leaving very little if anything in the cup for myself.

After living and working in NYC for a year, I learned my grandfather had fallen ill, so I moved to Atlanta to work retail and be close to my family. This was where I met my husband, Chris, after a couple of years of poor dating choices and living paycheck to paycheck through various retail gigs. Chris is kind, hardworking, and wildly intentional. He has a kind of honesty that stopped me in my tracks when we met because it was so pure and undiluted without being brutal. When we started dating I soon learned that Chris held me accountable and expected me to do what I said I was going to do. To that point, most men had just accepted what I said because it sounded nice. This forced me to grow up and understand that you can have a beautiful relationship and beautiful life when you do the work. Sometimes that work is hard because it's unfamiliar, but most times it's demanding because it requires a constant effort to maintain the relationship's goodness.

It took me a while to realize that the good results and good things that were happening in other people's lives weren't simply because they wished for them, but because they put in the necessary work. Nowadays, in this social media, hustle-hard, 24/7 news cycle, entrepreneurial-driven world, we're made to believe that the work gives instant results, especially if you have a lot of followers. You see no-nonsense messages online to "do the work" if in fact you want to make it in your professional life. "Ask for more and expect more to get more" is what they say online and in professional development books. But so many people expect their personal lives just to fall into place, and that just doesn't happen. And it's not because anything is wrong with them (or with you). There was nothing wrong with me. However, the work just wasn't being done. Every day requires a deliberate effort to make MAGIC. The everyday effort is the MAGIC.

I use the acronym MAGIC as a framework in this book, but by magic, I don't mean a trick, illusion, or even a hack. MAGIC is the discipline of showing up and doing the work to make every day:

Meaningful

Aesthetically pleasing

Goal-oriented

Intentional

Consistent

Creating everyday MAGIC takes work—not sporadically, once in a while, or when it's convenient work. It takes showing up every day to do work that matters to you on a consistent basis and that brings you closer to your goals in an intentional way. You can do that without sacrificing what you deem beautiful or trying to be everything to everyone.

What my friend's coworker seemed to believe was that to make every day MAGIC meant you needed to be an anomaly—the first, the only, the best. That's simply not true. Living a regular, everyday life where you do the necessary work to take care of yourself, your family, your home, and build a life that matters to you is MAGIC. MAGIC doesn't require a million followers or dollars. It also doesn't require you to shrink or play small. It doesn't mean you're supposed to be everything to everyone. It requires you to understand that you're more than enough. Everyday MAGIC requires honesty, openness, understanding, and confidence as you walk your own path. You will discover your everyday MAGIC when you're willing to do the work on purpose daily, not just when it's convenient or comfortable.

My life radically changed the moment I discovered my MAGIC. I thrive day to day because I do the work to make each and every day MAGIC. And you can too.

The entire point of making every day MAGIC is to make every day matter. It's the result and sum of the parts of what you want every day to be. Every day doesn't need to be perfect to matter. It just needs to have MAGIC. Your MAGIC helps you discover your joy and peace every single day, even on tough days, helping you remember that you don't have to be everything to everyone and that you're more than enough as you are. The everyday MAGIC framework helps you shift your mindset and shape your perspective, so you thrive on both the good days and those inevitable hard days. Everyday MAGIC is the method to the madness that daily life can often bring. Let's break down what each part of the framework means and how to apply it to your everyday life.

M IS FOR MEANINGFUL

So how do you make every day meaningful? When something is meaningful to you, it matters to you. Whether the meaning of something is sentimental, nostalgic, or something else is up to you. The goal is to take action and make decisions that matter to you on an everyday basis. When you practice making your everyday matter, you essentially create a life that matters to you. Often we make the mistake of believing that because something is a good idea or a good practice, we should make space for it in our lives. However, if something lacks meaning or purpose in your life, it will always stick out and be in the way. Understanding your why and knowing why certain routines, practices, and processes are present every day in your life will help you build a life that matters to you. The great news is, this is only up to you.

A IS FOR AESTHETICALLY PLEASING

Making every day aesthetically pleasing will look different for everyone. This is so important to understand because what's aesthetically pleasing to you isn't necessarily the case for others, and it doesn't need to be. When you surround yourself with things you deem beautiful every day, you appreciate and value them, which in turn helps you value yourself as well. You've probably heard the saying "You are the company you keep." The things you consider aesthetically pleasing within your vicinity—art, decor, objects, photography, and so on—are your company too.

G IS FOR GOAL-ORIENTED

We often see the hashtag #goals on social media when someone does or achieves something great. However, making every day goal-oriented isn't about trying to achieve something big and audacious on a daily basis. It's about remembering what matters to you on this particular day in this particular season in your life. Vague goals get vague results. Having specific goals—whether it's completing the five things on your to-do list, moving for thirty minutes every day, or having a dry January—helps you win. It's impossible to score without a goal, and having goals to work toward creates focus, momentum, and purpose for every single day.

I IS FOR INTENTIONAL

Intentionality is important because we often lead busy yet undisciplined lives. Making every day intentional requires decisiveness to make it count in a personalized way. It's not deep, just deliberate.

C IS FOR CONSISTENT

How do you create an everyday life you can look forward to? With consistency. Being consistent is hard and inconvenient in most cases because routines and processes can be mundane and boring. However, consistency makes space for you to develop new habits and creates a foundation for you to accomplish goals—whether they're short-term or lifelong. Sure, being consistent requires deliberate discipline and practice, which is often uncomfortable, but it breeds a level of self-confidence that's unmatched thanks to the results it produces.

There are a few ways you can use this book to make sure you get the most out of it. This is absolutely a "take the meat and leave the bone" kind of book. As you read, take what you need and leave what you don't.

You and I may be alike in many ways, but we're likely very different in many ways as well. I want you to always honor yourself: Use what works for you and leave behind what doesn't. There's a lot of stuff in here that was written with the intent to help you thrive day to day, but if what I share doesn't apply to your current situation, season, or life period, it's fine to skip it and keep moving.

There are sections in this book that act as rest stops or opportunities to go a little deeper in the cases when something does resonate with you:

MAGIC Memo

A quick note where a point is elaborated to create a deeper understanding.

MAGIC but Real

A quick confession where I admit how human I am and the compromises I make for peace of mind.

MAGIC Moment

A quick story about a moment from my real life where everyday MAGIC was clearly exemplified. Stories have a powerful way of making you understand a point through another's experience (versus just explaining it).

You can read this book from the first page to the last page, word for word, or you can skim it to find what you need. In either case, I encourage you to use it. There is nothing more MAGIC than applying what works for you. *Everyday MAGIC* was written to encourage you to discover things—old or new to you—that help you thrive on a day-to-day basis. Here you won't be shamed or lectured for not doing something a certain way. This also isn't the book that will "fix" you or turn you into a "superwoman."

Superwoman. That's what an innocent follower called me once as she commented on a photo of me with my kids on Instagram. Of course, I wasn't upset by it, but it certainly made me think about once upon a time when I used to try to be my own version of a superwoman.

It was a very played-out version, by the way.

I used to go to work, try to always say the right thing, decorate the house, dress my kids perfectly, have dinner on the table, and impress the people around me (or on the internet). This definition of a superwoman was all in my head, of course. No one ever told me that was required of me. I just assumed it was required of everyone. Usually, I'd end up being late no matter what, but I'd never ask for help, which often caused miscommunication with my husband, burning dinner, and then being too exhausted to willingly and patiently be with my kids. It was a vicious cycle. But that's exactly what happens when you try to do everything. You were never designed to do everything. So, trying to is a misuse of God's creation.

The problem with being everything to everyone is that you end up being nothing for yourself. What's in your cup is for you; the overflow is for everyone else. You cannot serve from an empty cup, though day to day as women that's how we try to operate. We're running on fumes because we want to please our families, grow our following on social media, increase our income at work or in our business, be a good friend, and not disappoint others. That sounds good, but it feels overwhelming in almost all cases. I know this because I've tried to do everything, be there for everyone else, thinking it would make me feel whole and complete—because I pleased others. But it didn't.

When you take away the money, the job, the business, the spouse, the kids, the friends, the followers, and all of the other things, what are you?

You're already complete.

No one or nothing else completes you. The meaning of complete is to have all the necessary or appropriate parts. You already have all the necessary parts to become the version of yourself you've always wanted to be. Your completeness makes you suitable to enter any room and able to reach any level you strive for. God makes no accidents—He intentionally made you complete.

I'm married to the most incredible man I've ever met, yet he does not complete me. Neither do my kids. Or my seven-figure business. Or my remarkable friends. I am complete and have been complete since the moment I was born. And so are you.

Of course, who you were as an infant and who you are as an adult are different versions of you. You were complete in both cases, just in different phases. When you change from who you once were to who you have become, it's not because you lacked anything; you're simply in a different phase.

Let's say your completeness is represented by a set of LEGO bricks. For this example, it's impossible to lose any of the pieces. However, your completeness doesn't reflect every type of LEGO ever created. Just enough to create a complete shape or structure. Here's the cool thing about LEGO sets: You can take them apart and rebuild them into something else. The pieces don't change, just their position and function. And the longer you have those pieces, the better you know how to use them. This is what happens as you grow in your completeness—you have that same set of LEGO bricks and you've built a stronger and sounder structure with fewer pieces. And now you have completeness with some pieces left over. So you no longer have just enough pieces; rather, you have more than enough.

That's exactly what you are. You're more than enough.

Your duty is to take the pieces of your completeness and build a life worth living. A life worth living makes everyday MAGIC.

Friends and followers often ask, "How do you do it all?" I don't. That's the MAGIC.

I'm not good at cooking on the fly, but I'm great at meal planning.

I don't like doing household chores, so I'm great at batching them.

I'm not good at remembering self-care, but I'm great at scheduling it.

I don't like forgetting what I have to do, so I'm great at writing it down.

I'm not good at managing a lot of stuff, but I'm great at purging regularly.

Others think I'm doing everything because I give my all to the things I am doing. I give them my completeness. However, they don't see all the things I'm not doing. And they don't see the work that went into making conscious decisions that ensure everything in my life is meaningful, aesthetically pleasing, goal-oriented, intentional, and consistent. They see the things I've chosen to do because they fit my framework.

You deserve a really good life, but you are not entitled to it. You will have to work harder than you expected on an everyday basis and shift the pieces of your life to adjust to the appropriate seasons. But the beauty of everyday MAGIC is that it's always relevant. Something will always be meaningful to you. Something will always be considered aesthetically pleasing to you. You will always have goals—whether they're big or small. Intentionality will always matter. And being consistent always pays off in the long run.

God's creation of you was meaningful. You were fearfully and wonderfully made.

You are aesthetically pleasing in His eyes.

His goal was to make you complete and that goal was accomplished. This is why He made you in His image—He is not an incomplete God. He lacks nothing—neither do you.

He was absolutely intentional and deliberate when He created you. Which is why He knows the plans He's made for you.

And He consistently pours blessings into your life whenever you make space for Him. Those plans He has for you? They're to prosper you. And He has. He does. And He will do so even more. That's not an opinion. It is the truth.

Whenever you come to a place where you're conflicted and trying to be everything to everyone, remember the MAGIC HAT. It's your "abracadabra-ask"—how to figure out whether or not something is for you.

A relationship.

A job opportunity.

A business proposition.

A life goal.

There are many things that are meaningful, aesthetically pleasing, goal-oriented, intentional, and consistent, but you have to ask, does it:

Honor you?

Apply to you?

Teach you?

HONOR YOU

If a MAGIC thing makes you feel seen, safe, heard, valued, and respected, you should pull it out of your hat and put it in your life. All things, from a job to a relationship, must honor your completeness. Something that honors you also fulfills you; and if the MAGIC thing doesn't, put it back in the hat. There's no space for it in your life, or at least, not in your current season.

APPLY TO YOU

Running a marathon is a goal many people have. It physically challenges you and gets you in great shape. You have to train consistently to do it well and it requires a lot of effort. It's a great goal to have—if it applies to you. If you want to run a marathon, it applies. If you don't, it doesn't. There are many things in life that you'll come across that work for others but don't work for you. If something isn't relevant to what you want, what you do, or who you want to be, that's fine. The goal here is to be explicitly honest with yourself about whether or not something actually applies to you. Self-honesty will always be your compass.

TEACH YOU

When things are challenging and even difficult, we often want to walk away from them because they're hard. But completing hard things is typically where we are taught new lessons and skills—both personally and professionally. Granted, strife isn't something to normalize in your everyday MAGIC—but learning is. If a new chapter in your life or even a new person is teaching you something and forcing you to grow, embrace the experience. Again, this is where self-honesty comes in, and it will certainly let you know if you should pull this out of your hat or keep it where you found it. The beauty of this is that only you can decide.

If something you're considering doesn't honor you, apply to you, and teach you, then it doesn't get to come out of the hat and into your life. It only comes out of the hat if it's MAGIC. That's the rule. Whatever MAGIC is out there must honor, apply to, and teach you. If not, it's not for you. No need for FOMO; what's meant for you will not miss you.

I'll be honest: Before I discovered everyday MAGIC, I used to get paranoid whenever things were going well in my life. For some reason, I felt that I didn't deserve that good fortune, and I lived with a sense of inevitable doom as I waited for it all to be taken away.

I'm here to tell you, that's not how any of this works. That's not how God works. God wants you to have good. He wants you to have a lot of good. And He wants you to have it every day.

It's scary when you're trusted with a lot. When I pray, I sometimes ask, *Respectfully, are You sure, Lord?* And He always reminds me that He trusts me, so why shouldn't I trust myself?

And yes, you, too, should trust yourself enough to make MAGIC, every day.

Everyday MAGIC isn't a destination, it's a journey. The process requires being present, doing the work, and still being joyful while the work is getting done. That's right: joy and work—they can coincide. That's the whole point of everyday MAGIC. It's not that the work gets easier, it's just that you have learned to get out of your own way and are now truly grateful to do the work.

Getting out of our own way is an extreme sport. It requires explicit honesty and acute self-awareness that make most of us uncomfortable. But if you stand flat-footed and answer the hard questions, I promise you that there's good stuff underneath and you'll discover that every day can be meaningful, aesthetically pleasing, goal-oriented, intentional, and consistent.

Now that you know what everyday MAGIC is, let's discover how to make it your own.

EVERYDAY
MAGIC

CHAPTER ONE

The MAGIC of Discovering Why

Always start with why.

Early on in our marriage, before we had kids, I tried to become this person in my mind who was good at routines and good at being domesticated. I'd try to cook and then clean and then cater to my husband, who would look at me like, "Why are you doing all of this?" Chris never asked me to do any of those things, by the way. I'd get overwhelmed when things wouldn't happen perfectly and apologize to my husband for a version of me he never even asked for. All because

I was trying to be this "ideal" version of myself and arrive at the situational destinations of everyday life perfectly.

I had this really outdated version of being a wife and mom in my head. Can you relate? Cook, clean, be agreeable, and make it all seem effortless—I told myself that this was what others expected of me when in fact it was a lie I told myself and continued to believe for whatever reason.

Emulating something you've seen a fictional character do on television or someone else in real life do because you think you're not enough will always dilute your true purpose. I learned this the hard way.

Many of those times, I wore myself out with trying to be something I wasn't simply because I wasn't being honest with myself. I wasn't honest about who I was or who I wanted to be. I was so focused on external opinions—*What did Chris think about this? What would my mom think? Would my friends be impressed?*

I was bombarding myself with opinions that (1) didn't matter; and (2) didn't even exist.

The reason I wasn't being honest with myself was because I hadn't decided who I wanted to be and why I wanted to be her.

Oftentimes when you don't know what you want or why you want it, it's easier to simply try to please others so if you come up short, you can put it on them and their expectations. It's a cop-out with a pretty people-pleasing bow on it.

Discovering your calling is an ongoing journey that requires a lifetime to fully realize. It is not a picture-perfect destination where you will arrive knowing all the answers. Here's one thing I know for sure: your purpose in life cannot be to please others. Sure, it's great to serve others and even to help them. And if you happen to please others as a result of doing what's best for you, that's totally fine. But when pleasing people becomes the sole pursuit of how you live your day-to-day life, it will always be disappointing.

If I'm going to please anyone besides myself, I aim to please God with how I take care of myself, treat others, and live my life. I think it's the least I can do since He created me and He means the most to me. That requires me to deliberately say yes or no to certain things. It's not always easy, but what makes your purpose clear is deciding your why.

ENVISION YOUR LIFE WITH PURPOSE

Your purpose is your why. It's the foundation of the decisions you make, the actions you take, and the life you lead. It's the core of why you say yes or no. It's your internal GPS. It gives your life direction. Many people are so focused on speed in life but are headed nowhere, and it has nothing to do with their being a nobody. It's just that they have no direction. Before you can dive into discovering your everyday MAGIC, your why has to be apparent. When you're clear on your why, then you'll make everyday MAGIC on purpose. To get clear on your purpose you have to envision your life with purpose. Then you'll be able to ask yourself daily:

Why is today meaningful to me?
How can I make today aesthetically pleasing?

Have I made today goal-oriented?
Are my efforts today intentional?
Am I being consistent today?

Not only will you be able to answer those questions clearly, but the answers will matter to you and you'll know what you'll give your time to. What leads to our being overwhelmed in our everyday lives is doing a bunch of things that take up a lot of our time but that have no purpose in our lives.

If your everyday life is a painting, everyday MAGIC is the paint, and your why is the canvas. This is why the days you lose sight of your canvas (your why) and are just throwing around paint (your MAGIC) turn out to be nothing but a mess no matter how well you try to throw the paint. Because what's the point of painting with no canvas?

Discovering your why requires clear vision, explicit honesty, and deliberate decisiveness—about who you are, where you want to be, what you want, and why you want it. That requires patience, perspective, and planning.

Who are you? What are your strengths? What are your opportunities
    of growth?
Where are you in your life right now? Where would you like to be in
    the future?
What do you really want out of life? Are you willing to do the work
    for it daily?
Why do you want this life? What greater purpose does your life serve?

These questions are worth taking a moment to pause and answer in a journal or even your Notes app. No one other than you has the answers. There are no right or wrong answers. However, to get the clarity necessary to joyfully yet purposefully navigate everyday life, answering these questions is helpful. Also, your answers can change over time and likely will. When you grow, you will change and so will the perspective of your purpose and the flow of your everyday life. Not only is that okay, it's expected.

Before you have the life you want, you have to see it. It's true what they say: You have to see it to believe it. Even if it's only in your mind, visualizing what your life looks like with MAGIC and purpose gives you permission to have it and go get it.

MAGIC MEMO

Get a small notebook or start a Google document and call it: "The [Your Name] Manifesto." Putting your name on something is powerful—it gives you ownership. Then find a quiet place where there will be no interruptions for ten minutes. Close your eyes and imagine what the most MAGIC day looks like for you. Start your visualization with you sitting in the movie theater. The movie is called *Everyday MAGIC*, starring you. In the movie, you're going to have the most MAGIC day. The movie starts, and the camera reveals your home and starts to move toward your bedroom. You stand up in the theater and walk toward the screen. When you touch the screen, you magically enter the scene and the movie starts with you waking up. What does your room look like? What kind of pajamas are you wearing? How do you feel? Then go on with your day. What do you see when you look in the mirror? What do you put on for the day? When you walk into the kitchen, what do you decide to eat? How does the food taste? If you have a family, what kind of mood is everyone in? Is there music playing in the background? Leave no detail to chance. Interact with your family while eating and enjoying your meal. Once you're done eating, walk to a quiet part of your home where you can sit and write. As you walk, you see photos on the wall of amazing life moments with loved ones and friends. When you sit down, you write a letter to yourself. In the letter, you explain how you were able to achieve this MAGIC day. You share the tasks and habits that matter most, why you dress and decorate the way you do, the routines that you're intentional about, and how you stay consistent on the days you don't feel like it. When you're done writing the letter, you tell your family you'll be right back. You put the letter in an envelope and put your shoes on. When you open the door, it's actually the screen back to the movie theater. When you walk through the door, you're back in the movie theater. Open your eyes and write the letter you wrote yourself in your *Everyday MAGIC* movie.

This letter will act as a permission slip to have MAGIC in your day-to-day life. Then write down why you want this MAGIC daily. Why is the day you visualized important to you? The answer to that question is your why. You can reference it and edit it as you see fit. Also, you won't have the pressure of having to remember every little detail of your why and your MAGIC because you have a document that reminds you. Sure, you might think that if it's so important to you you should automatically know or remember all of it, but you already have so much to remember. The kids' after-school schedule, your next dentist appointment, what your boss emailed you about this morning, and what's for dinner tonight. There is no shame in creating a document that details everything you hope to attain during your journey of personal growth.

Start with the visualization first and then answer the following questions the best you can. It's not about the answers being perfect, but more about your being decisive and answering the questions honestly. Again, it doesn't have to be deep, just deliberate. Don't worry about being right or wrong, just decide on your answers. You can always change your why later. Remember, your why is your GPS; it gives your life direction. Even when the destination changes (getting married, buying a home, getting a new job, getting divorced, having kids, etc.), direction always matters.

Who are you? What are your strengths? What are your opportunities of growth?

Where are you in your life right now? Where would you like to be in the future?

What do you really want out of life? Are you willing to do the work for it daily?

Why do you want this life? What greater purpose does it serve?

If you were to stop and answer those questions right now, what would your answers be?

Stop now, set a timer for ten minutes, visualize your MAGIC day, and answer those questions so you can start the discovery of your why in your manifesto document. Why ten minutes? Because it's long enough to be thoughtful but short enough to create a sense of urgency and encourage decisiveness.

YOUR MISSION STATEMENT

In the early days of my marriage, I wasn't honest with myself about the season I was in. I also wasn't being decisive about what I wanted. When I look back now, I realize I should've decided to enjoy being married and being in our home early on in our marriage. In that season, I totally lacked perspective because I was too busy wishing the grass were greener. We didn't have kids or many responsibilities, so that was a time to really relish it just being the two of us and deciding who I wanted to be. Not only did I lack perspective, but I lacked decisiveness. I lacked the decision making required to decide my why and make everyday MAGIC on purpose.

No two seasons in your life will ever be the same. Five years from now when my kids are thirteen, nine, and seven, it will feel different in our house because everyone will be potty-trained and doing chores. Just like ten years ago, when it was just me and Chris in our first house, trying to figure out life, it was way different. Both seasons are equally valuable. Good seasons are valuable just like hard seasons, because the work still has to get done and the why still matters. Trust me, when you're going through hell, you want direction on how to get out fast. That requires decisiveness and knowing your why.

After two years of struggle, Chris and I separated, and when we got back together, we went to therapy. (I highly suggest therapy if you're married, even if you're not struggling.) A few weeks after Chris and I reconciled following being separated for three months, we went to counseling and therapy to really learn about ourselves. It was a hard but necessary process. Part of our "work" when we got back together was to define our why. Being married is a lot of work. Having a family is also. However, I believe it's worth it. I'm not really sure where we got the idea that a life worth having would be easy or even effortless. Everything I've ever wanted in my life has been a lot more work than I imagined, my marriage and family life included. To get the job you want, you have to put together a résumé that explains the skills and experience you have. To start a business, you should have a business plan—a document that contains your mission statement and plans for the future.

Interestingly, we don't do these types of things for our personal lives. However, I believe we should.

This is why I decided to create my own personal mission statement. I can't lie, this seemed like a heavy and major task in the beginning. If I got it wrong, I was convinced that my life would be doomed, so I avoided it. But the longer I dragged my feet on deciding my life's mission, the harder my everyday life was. I was pretending to be myself instead of actually being my most authentic self on purpose. It overwhelmed me until I sat down one day and simply decided to do it.

Here's the secret—your life's mission is simple. It's meaningful because it's a specific mission designed exclusively for you, but still—it's simple. That's probably what's holding you back, like it held me back. I thought I had to write out a deep, King James Version thesis of my life when the truth is a mission is simply an assignment.

What is the assignment you want to fulfill with your life? If you're being honest with yourself, what does your own personal mission statement look like?

You get to design the life you want. A personal mission statement gives you space and permission to understand the assignment and then complete it with the efforts of your life.

When I sat down, prayed, reflected, let my mind wander, and daydreamed about the life I wanted, this is the personal mission statement I came up with:

To honor God by living well and creating an everyday life I love and appreciate.

I enjoy traveling and I love celebrating special moments like birthdays and holidays. However, I didn't want those to be the only times I loved and appreciated my life. I want to enjoy my life every day and live well on purpose to show the Lord that the life He gave me really matters to me. So I flourish in it every day in small and big ways.

After praying about this and leading my day-to-day life in a way that fulfills the assignment, I know for sure that this is my personal mission in life.

The amazing thing about creating your personal mission statement is that it ends up being the base of any other mission statements in your life. My personal mission statement has noticeably influenced both my family mission statement and my company's mission statement.

At The Mattie James Company, our mission statement is:

To create content, products, and experiences that encourage women to thrive in their everyday lives and take the mysticism out of living well.

You see, my personal mission statement and my company's mission statement are siblings. Not twins—as they shouldn't be—but certainly related. Whether you're an entrepreneur or work a day job, I believe that everyone should rely on their personal mission statement to determine how they work and why.

Having a family mission statement has created a clarity for me that I didn't have early on in my marriage and when I started having kids. Writing down your goals and purpose as a family matters because it gives you something to work toward in the most important group you'll likely ever be a part of. Sure, motherhood and marriage should be important if they matter to you, but having a family mission gives them a personalized purpose.

I understand that having kids and getting married don't matter to everyone. That's fine. But a family mission statement can be for a married couple without kids, because you're still a family. It can certainly be for single parents with kids, because, again, you're a family. A family mission statement isn't reserved for what you think your family is supposed to be; it's for your family as it is. It's something for your family to actively work toward—it's not some ideal to try to hurriedly attain; it's an active mission of becoming.

Our family mission statement is something that we agreed to when we reconciled after our separation before our last two kids were born. Essentially, it's the why for our family. Our family mission statement is:

To bring joy and light to our community through freedom of expression in Christ.

If it ain't attached to joy and light, then it's not for my family. If it doesn't allow us to express freely through Christ, then it's not for our family. The family mission statement is a standard that allows us to say, "Hey, we want to be a part of it" or "That's not for us." Community has always been important to us because we know that it takes a village. We see how instrumental that was in our lives early on, in both my and Chris's childhoods. So it was important to make sure that our family mission statement reflected that.

When you sit down to decide what your personal mission statement is, take your time and be bold with it. This is your opportunity to decide how you want to live your life. While that can be hard, it's also exciting. That's how much power you have—you are the one who gets to make that decision. Keep it short, straight to the point, and simple.

When you think about how you want to live out your life, what's the first thing that comes to mind?

What do you do now (even if it's a small thing) on an everyday basis that you enjoy and believe you would continue to do even five years from now?

Based on who you see yourself becoming, what's the mission you must carry out no matter what?

Answer the questions above and then write out your personal mission statement in your manifesto document. Try your best to make your mission statement one straight-to-the-point sentence.

It's best to think about creating your mission statement when you're rested and at ease. Be wildly intentional about that. You must have the right heart and mindset when you're coming up with your why. I understand that getting eight full hours of sleep may not be your style or even readily available to you in the current season of your life. (I know with three small children, six to seven hours a night is the best I can do.) You also want to be hydrated to think clearly. (For me, caffeine gives me a necessary boost.) Last, schedule an uninterrupted hour (away from others and away from your phone) to just let your mind truly wander as you consider what your personal mission statement is. Always start with why. This can be done before the kids get home from school, during a lunch break sitting in your car, or even on a weekend at the library in one of those private rooms. Write down honest and organic answers at first and then tweak after you're done.

MAKE IT MAGIC

Okay, so you have an idea of what your why is now that you have a personal mission statement. How do you make discovering your why—aka your personal mission statement—MAGIC?

First, you want to decide what is most meaningful to you in your life. Living well is meaningful to me because it's my way of honoring God with the life He's given me. My personal mission statement matters to me because it is specific and personal to me. Part of the MAGIC of discovering your why is deciding what really matters to you.

Chris and I—and honestly, all of our kids as well—are creative, and having the space to freely express our creativity is deeply meaningful to us. But what's most important to us is that when we create, we do it in a way that when others see what we've created or what we're a part of, they inevitably see God. That's how we want to move collectively and individually as a family.

If I'm not living well, then I'm missing the mark personally. If we're not adding joy and light to our community, our tribe, or our village, then we've missed the mark. If we're not encouraging women to thrive in their everyday lives, then we're missing the mark as a company.

You will miss the mark sometimes because you're human. Your personal mission statement isn't a declaration for you to be perfect. It's an assignment where God gets to use you as an imperfect vessel to do remarkable things. When you do miss the mark, step back, forgive yourself, refocus, and get back on your assignment.

While your personal mission statement isn't a physical thing, you must consider it beautiful. When you daydream about carrying out this life assignment of yours, it should excite you. In a way, you can imagine it as the trailer of your life's mission. It should be the movie you saw in your visualization. That's how you make discovering your why aesthetically pleasing.

Once you decide what your why is, line up most of—if not all of—your goals with your personal mission statement. The reason your why is so powerful is because it starts to make sense of the laundry list of goals you have. A lot of the goals we have are rooted in what others are doing, what they think we should be doing, or what we've told ourselves to do to be considered "enough." If you already have a list of goals, take a look at it again after you come up with your personal mission statement.

Are these goals actually in alignment with your why? How can you tweak your existing goals to line up with your personal mission statement? Do you need to come up with completely new goals?

Last, after you discover your why, consistently go in the direction that your why is guiding you. To keep yourself on track, reference your personal manifesto and what you've written. There will be days that are hard, stressful, and really test your limits. When you think about your personal mission statement on those hard days, it should reset your heart and focus your mind. It will remind you why you're so committed to designing a life that matters to you.

A personal mission statement gives you guidance and direction in how you operate as a person. A family mission statement does the same for a family. My personal mission statement has allowed me to trust myself more in the decisions I make and why I make them. It has helped me understand the assignment. My prayer is that our family mission is a seed to produce fruit in our children's lives as they grow up, design their lives, get married, and have their own families. I believe that personal and family mission statements are a road map to building a family legacy and creating generational blessings.

Discovering and deciding your why by designing your own personal mission statement truly helps navigate your everyday MAGIC by creating a purposeful foundation. It is without question one of the most meaningful things you'll ever do. I encourage you to take time out within the next twenty-four hours to do so in your personal manifesto while it's fresh in your mind after reading this chapter.

CHAPTER TWO

Health Is MAGIC

Self-care is healthcare.

As I'm writing this, I'm on a twenty-four-hour self-care and writing day. My amazing sister, Maya, surprised and treated me to it. A hotel suite, a fifty-minute massage, and twenty-four uninterrupted hours to myself. It feels good.

Now, to some people being away from your family for twenty-four hours seems like a lot. There's mom-guilt, and the micromanaging we do of everything that happens at home and work, and the inevitable second-guessing question: Is this really necessary?

For me, it is.

The truth is that for most of us, getting time to ourselves is very necessary. Being accessible to someone else 24/7 is taxing. No one should have 24/7 access to you. You are a person, not property. You're allowed to take a break, even take a long bath or mental health day if need be. Does this mean you can neglect your family and other life responsibilities? Of course not. Needing and craving uninterrupted alone time doesn't mean you love your family any less or that you've all of a sudden become an irresponsible person. It just means you need a break. A moment of stillness. Stillness is self-care. And self-care is nonnegotiable because it's part of your health.

MAGIC BUT REAL

Twenty-four hours is a lot of time to be away from your family, especially if you don't have family or friends nearby to hold down your home base as you take time for yourself. If your schedule won't allow you to have a literal day to yourself, take a few hours. Take a personal day or use your day off to intentionally relax while your kids are at school or the baby is with a loved one. This "you day" could end up being six to eight hours (rather than a full twenty-four hours), but because your time was intentionally uninterrupted and reserved for you to recenter and relax, it still serves its purpose. Put your phone on "Do Not Disturb," delete social media to prevent scrolling, let your village know that you'll be unavailable unless it's an

emergency, and do whatever recharges you. Give yourself
permission to do so. Be encouraged to take a "you day"
at least once a month or quarter (depending on your
schedule).

Just because your children and spouse aren't stuck on you 24/7
doesn't mean that you aren't doing a good job as a mother and/or wife.
We all need space to be—just simply be—so when it is time to live,
work, be productive, and be present that can happen fully. Requiring
space isn't a shortcoming or being selfish, it's being human—which is
required to be healthy.

If you have kids, stop using motherhood as an excuse not to take
care of yourself. Not only is it a disservice to you, it's a disservice to
your kids. Anytime you are not prioritizing your physical, emotional,
mental, and spiritual health, you're showing your kids that it's fine to
put other people and things above one's health for the sake of saving
face. How our children view and value health is a behavior they learn
at home.

Be honest. Based on how you take care of yourself, what's the
health lesson you're currently teaching to your children?

Health is what so many of us are putting on the back burner
because we "just don't have the time." Well, let me tell you something: you'd better make time for health or the lack of good health
will force you to. I say this as someone who isn't usually excited about
her morning workout—I'm definitely the girl who would rather eat

a slice of pound cake instead of broccoli. However, when I choose discipline over comfort and I do knock out my morning strength-training session, I feel like a million bucks. The workout helps me not only physically, but also mentally and emotionally, which ends up setting the tone for the day.

Health is MAGIC and you have to make space for MAGIC every single day. There are layers to your health, which we'll discuss in a minute, but I encourage you to prioritize your health while it's a preventative measure versus a recovery method. They say, "An ounce of prevention is worth a pound of cure." Putting your health first now before anything is wrong is crucial because it's so much harder to recover from health issues. But either way, you can have what it takes to do the work to take care of yourself physically, mentally, emotionally, and spiritually.

MAGIC MEMO

What is health? According to Dictionary.com, health is "the state of being free of illness or injury." Health is freedom. Anytime you prioritize keeping yourself in good health, you prioritize keeping yourself free.

Let's be clear, good health isn't just exercise and eating clean. Those are parts of your physical health. Your health is a sum of your physical, emotional, mental, and spiritual conditions, and your self-care includes the maintenance of all four layers of health.

It's important to prioritize your health daily to make your health MAGIC.

SELF-CARE

Self-care is meaningful maintenance. It's the practice of taking action to preserve or improve one's own health. I truly believe that you must practice self-care every day to maintain good health.

For clarity, self-care isn't the overly indulgent shopping spree after a mani-pedi like TV and movies have sold it to be. It is a discipline that requires you to show up for yourself deliberately in some version every single day.

What I've learned is that being present consistently cannot happen without being still intentionally.

Another thing that must be pointed out is that self-care takes time. This is why most of us try to skip it, because we tell ourselves the lie of not having enough time. It's not true. You do have enough time—for the things that matter. But the other lie you have to stop telling yourself is that everything matters. Because it doesn't. Different things will matter in different seasons. Your job is to be explicitly honest with yourself about which things matter now.

At this moment, walking or moving daily for at least thirty minutes, taking care of and spending time with my family, getting this book manuscript to my editor in the next three weeks, and fulfilling my contracted duties with brand partners are my priorities. This will look different next quarter when the book is written and other things come up.

Taking care of myself is something that everyone around me is familiar with because it's a life priority. Every Friday afternoon I have therapy for an hour. I'm known to get a massage like I did today more often than not throughout the year. I pray and read the Word. I exercise even on days I don't feel like it. I eat green vegetables a couple of times a day. All of that is part of self-care.

Self-care is your wellness free will, stress management, and commitment to your wholeness for the sake of health and peace of mind. So yes, it takes time. Because self-care matters, you make time for it. You've probably told yourself, "I'd like to have time for self-care, but I don't have enough time."

When was the last time you scheduled self-care?

You say you don't have the time, but you simply haven't scheduled it. Making appointments for self-care is an arrangement to meet with yourself for a certain amount of time to take care of yourself accordingly. What you'll come to learn is that self-care is also best maintained through a variety of appointments on an annual, quarterly, monthly, and sometimes weekly basis. Here are the self-care appointments to make (and keep!) to improve your health and make a meaningful difference in your everyday:

Annual or Biannual Basis
General Practitioner

As long as you're in good health—meaning you don't have any major or chronic issues—you can see your general practitioner once a year. With that being said, don't miss that appointment. It's important to know what's going on in your body.

Dentist

Your teeth are important to your appearance. Not only that, but your oral health directly affects your heart health and so much more as well. The maintenance of your teeth, mouth, and gums is critical to your physical health. As long as you don't have any chronic or major issues, you should go to the dentist twice a year to get a deep cleaning and checkup.

Gynecologist

Let's talk about our lady parts and how we need to take care of them, shall we? At least once a year, you should see a gynecologist to ensure that you're healthy and have nothing to worry about.

It can certainly be an uncomfortable appointment to go to, so do your research and ask for recommendations from trusted family and friends when finding a gynecologist. It feels good knowing that you're taking care of yourself by knowing what's going on with your body. (A word on mammograms: unless you have a specific concern or issue, if you're age forty through fifty-four, you should get a mammogram screening every year, and after that, switch to every two years.)

Monthly or Quarterly Basis
Facial

A monthly or even quarterly facial can do wonders for your skin. It's a great way to get a deep clean of your pores and evaluate the current condition of your skin. Doing this with an aesthetician and getting their opinion as an expert is always a plus. I especially believe in doing this when you have a big moment in your life (wedding, special photos, etc.) coming up. If you're frugal like my bestie who can't imagine spending money on someone else "washing her face," then learn how to give yourself a facial at home. An at-home steamer and the right products can make a big difference in the health and appearance of your skin.

Massage

One of my favorite self-care appointments to make is for a massage. I wouldn't consider myself a massage snob by any means because I'm soft and I only want light to medium pressure. To me, even a light (or medium) massage can make a huge difference in posture, mindset, and stress. After getting my first massage, I realized how much tension I hold in my back and neck during really hectic or stressful moments in my life.

If you've never gotten a massage, I encourage you to try it at least once. I try to go every quarter, if not more frequently when I need it.

Sure, physical touch is not everything, but if you're a working human your feet likely get tired. If getting a massage is not for you, I have to suggest getting a back or foot massager. Those little machines are lifesavers after a really hard day. I use them in crunch times when I can't get in for a massage appointment.

Weekly or Biweekly Basis
Manicure + Pedicure

Even if you're not a girly girl, getting your nails and feet done is a nice self-care pampering activity that I believe most of us can enjoy.

It does take maintenance, since it usually must be done once or twice a month, but you can make it work for you. Whether you like a simple, modest manicure with your natural nails or over-the-top stiletto nails with all the nail art, it's a way to express yourself while getting your hands and feet tended to. Modest budget? No worries—open up Pinterest and choose your favorite nail inspo and have a go at it. A DIY manicure and pedicure is not only attainable but fun to do when you commit to polish and products you like.

Hair

Clean and healthy hair tends to contribute to clean and healthy skin. I admittedly don't like the task of washing and doing my hair— it always feels like a chore to me. However, once it's done I'm so glad I did it. If you really don't like caring for your hair, find a stylist you like and trust (it'll take some trial and error so take recommendations from friends and family) and make an appointment on a biweekly or monthly basis.

Therapy

I will dive deeper into this in a moment, but therapy is absolutely a part of your self-care. I go to both individual and couples therapy, which has been greatly beneficial to my health and life. But the individual therapy has made me more self-aware, gracious, and patient with myself, which in turn trickles down into every other relationship and aspect of my life. It's not solely a resource I go to when something is wrong. It's mental and emotional health maintenance, and when something needs to be maintained it's necessary to make time for it.

Daily
Sleep

You have to sleep. You must sleep. It's a nonnegotiable. When I don't sleep, I'm mean to my husband, my children, everyone around me, and myself. Put your phone down at night, girl, and get to bed.

Quiet Time

I'll get into specifics later on about quiet time and how I use it to my advantage, but I must say that sitting in nothing but quiet for even fifteen minutes a day can change your mood for the better. No phone, no talking to other people, just you and your thoughts for fifteen to sixty minutes a day is *huge*.

Skin-Care Routine

We're going to discuss your morning and evening skin-care routines and how imperative they are to your health—and why they're MAGIC—in the next section, but simply washing and moisturizing your face consistently is vital to your skin health. Clean skin is healthy skin and you and I and everyone else all want healthy skin.

No matter how you cut it, beauty is health and should be prioritized as such. When I say beauty, I don't mean just putting on makeup. Beauty usually entails maintaining the health of all things skin, hair, and nails.

Here's something that I've never admitted: Being beautiful matters to me. More specifically, being beautiful to myself matters to me. I was never the "pretty girl." I was always too skinny and underdeveloped and usually the token Black kid in all-white environments growing up. So even when I was deemed "pretty" to others, it was "for a Black girl." Couple that with adolescent acne, and being beautiful was never something that I believed I could actually be considered as.

From fifteen to seventeen, I had the worst acne. When you're a teenager, your hormones serve as a shaky foundation to your confidence, and my skin certainly didn't help mine. I felt insecure and hopeless. I'd never had issues with breakouts or any kind of skin issues before, but now I had officially reached the point of my life where washing my face with soap could no longer cut it. Several times after she got home from work, my mom would take me to the drugstore and we would decide what cleanser, toner, or moisturizer I should try to see if a product would be the right fit for me.

I tried Noxema. Too harsh.

I tried Cetaphil. Too mild.

I tried Clean & Clear. Dried up my skin.

I tried Neutrogena. Perfect.

But I had to use a toner and moisturizer as well.

Mommy always said that there's no such thing as an ugly person, just a lazy one. That sort of made sense to me then but makes a whole lot of sense now. You have to do the work to figure out what works (products, routines, procedures, etc.) for your skin and be consistent with it.

I felt insecure when my skin was bad as a teenager. Sometimes I still feel like that when my skin is just rearing its ugly head. Those times don't happen often, but usually when my skin isn't its best it's because I've been inconsistent with my skin-care routine.

When you look in the mirror at your own face, what do you see? Is it someone beautiful? Or do you immediately start an internal conversation about what could be different or better?

Here's what I know now—I am beautiful. Not only because I like what I look like on the outside, but because of how I treat myself. I put in the work intentionally to treat my skin and myself well.

MAGIC MEMO

Naturally, we all have insecurities and things we wish were different. However, I want you to stop looking at yourself and wishing something were different. Always start internal conversations with what you love about yourself. Treat yourself as someone who deserves to be loved—because you do. I love that society is currently working toward being more body-positive, no matter the shape or size of someone's body. What I want you to work on is being "you-positive." Genuinely celebrate and appreciate *you* always, even when there is room for improvement. As for those areas that you wish could be improved—not necessarily changed—look into doing the work necessary to achieve your desired result. Typically that work is finding the right product or routine that works best for your skin and body.

SKIN CARE

All skin is not the same, which is why it's not fair to look at your best friend's skin-care routine, copy it, and wonder why it's not working for you. You very likely don't have the same skin type or sensitivities as they do. Most people are familiar with two skin types—dry and oily. In reality there are five skin types:

- Normal
- Dry
- Oily
- Combination
- Sensitive

Think of your skin as a sponge. You don't want the sponge to be too dry, too oily, or too sensitive to use. You want it to absorb the right products without being compromised.

Here's a brief breakdown of each in case you don't know what your skin type is.

Normal skin is well-balanced; not too oily, not too dry. As a sponge, it is perfectly balanced and ready to absorb products.

If you have normal skin, your skin is just right. You don't err on the side of being too dry or too oily and your skin isn't sensitive to any ingredients. This doesn't mean normal skin is perfect—it may be bothered by minor dryness, blemishes, or oiliness, but only occasionally and barely detectable. Consider yourself blessed (and very much envied).

To maintain normal skin, it's best to keep it exfoliated with hydrating acids, nourished with antioxidants, and protected with SPF products.

MAGIC Ingredients: Vitamin C, AHAs, and SPF-30 (or greater) products.

Dry skin is rough, dull, or dehydrated. As a sponge, it is too dry to properly absorb products.

When you have dry skin, it typically looks dull and feels tight. This is a result of the skin not producing enough sebum (oil) in addition to being dehydrated and dead skin cells not being exfoliated.

To remedy dry skin, you should use products that hydrate (water), moisturize (oil), and help exfoliate without irritating the skin (as some acids can sometimes do).

MAGIC Ingredients: Lactic acid, ceramides, and squalene.

Oily skin has excess oil and is prone to acne or breakouts. As a sponge, it is too oily to properly absorb products.

Oily skin overproduces sebum and tends to be prone to breakouts because of excess oil. Pores are noticeably visible; skin feels greasy and looks shiny.

To remedy oily skin, you should use products that clear out the excess oil from pores, balance out the sebum production, and reduce the appearance of pores.

MAGIC Ingredients: Retinol, salicylic acid, and hyaluronic acid (in serum form).

Combination skin can be both dry and oily; the T-zone is the typically oily area. As a sponge, it is too dry and too oily in different spots to properly absorb products.

With combination skin, it's a matter of treating both the oily and the dry zones of your face accordingly. It may seem weird using two different masks or serums on your face, but with combination skin that's sometimes the best approach.

To resolve combination skin, you want to treat the problems appropriately starting with gently exfoliating dead skin cells. You also want to use products that eliminate excess oil with balancing ingredients while moisturizing and hydrating the dry areas.

MAGIC Ingredients: BHAs, AHAs, and antioxidants.

Sensitive skin is prone to inflammation, irritation, and redness. As a sponge, it overreacts if you don't use mild and gentle products.

Sensitive skin is just that—skin that is sensitive. The wrong products will make it overreact to the point of redness, inflammation, or breakouts. It's more delicate than any other skin type and should be treated as such. It still needs to be consistently cleansed, exfoliated, and moisturized, but with milder yet effective ingredients.

To remedy sensitive skin, you want to use soothing and nutrient-rich products that help you achieve great results. Aim to use ingredients that keep the skin calm, clear out acne/irritation, and nourish the skin barrier.

MAGIC Ingredients: Aloe, honey, and cucumber seed oil.

Determining your skin type is pretty simple with the bare face method. Simply wash your face with a mild foaming cleanser. Dry it and then don't put any other products on it. After twenty to thirty minutes, look at your skin to see how it feels and looks.

Does it feel tight and itchy?

Does it look shiny and feel greasy?

Does it feel both dry and oily?

Is it irritated or red at all?

Does it look and feel balanced?

After the bare face test, you should have a good idea of what skin type you have.

Once you know what your skin type is, it's important to keep that information in mind and create your skin-care routine using the right products.

The Core Four Products—Morning

Cleanser

Eye cream

Moisturizer

SPF coverage

The Core Four Products—Evening

Cleanser
Eye cream
Serum
Moisturizer

When you start your day with a clean face, you hit the ground running in my opinion. For those of us who wear makeup, makeup absolutely looks better on clean skin. Now, if you're just getting started with establishing a morning skin-care routine, begin with cleanser.

For your morning cleanser, you want something mild that gently cleanses your skin. Regardless of skin type, a foaming or gel cleanser will certainly serve you because you don't need to deep clean in the morning. You'll likely just be removing your nighttime skin-care products. Especially if you're going to do makeup, you don't want to rile up your skin. A gentle cleanser will do.

I believe in eye cream in both the daytime and the nighttime. Always, always apply your eye cream with your ring finger, because it's the finger with the lightest pressure. Be sure to get under your eye and up to your orbital bone right beneath your eyebrow. If you're going to wear under-eye concealer, be sure to let the eye cream sit on your skin at least ten minutes before applying the concealer for best results.

Always moisturize your skin after you cleanse it. It instantly thanks you, especially if you use the right one. In your morning skin-care routine, you'll want something light yet moisturizing. If you have dry or normal skin, use a moisturizer that has a little more oil. If you have combination or oily skin, use a moisturizer that's more hydrating—that has more water. Either way, you want something that feels lightweight throughout the day.

Wear an SPF product every day. Every single day. No matter the season. No matter the weather. No matter your skin type. No matter your mood. In the winter, in the spring, in the summer, in the fall. When it's sunny, when it rains, when it snows, when it's cloudy. When you're inside or when you're outside. You don't have to see the sun for it to affect your skin. You wear an SPF product every single day. UV rays will damage your skin if you don't protect it.

I believe in sun protection so much that we're going to have a little lesson on it and what it protects you from so you know I'm not playing with you about wearing an SPF product every day.

There are two types of UV rays—UVA and UVB.

UVA rays cause aging.

UVB rays cause sunburn.

A is for aging.

B is for burn.

That's how I remember the two.

Typically, we pay attention to damage resulting from UVB rays because it's on the surface. But UVA rays are an aging villain. UVA rays destroy the collagen and elastin in your skin, causing wrinkles and almost all types of skin aging. This is the radiation used in tanning beds. (Yikes!) Here's the other wild thing about UVA rays: They account for 95 percent of the UV rays on earth's surface. Yeah, that's right: 95 PERCENT. They penetrate deep into your skin and break it down.

While UVB rays make up only 5 percent of the UV rays on earth and don't deeply affect the dermis like UVA, they do destroy the surface of your skin. Aside from damaging your skin cells and contributing to melanoma, they can also cause cataracts.

SPF stands for sun protection factor. Meaning products with SPF 50 protect you more than products with SPF 15. At the minimum, you want to wear products with an SPF of 30 to stay protected. My daily sunscreen is rated SPF 50, and on those days I'm directly out in the sun (which is not often), I apply and reapply hourly.

An SPF product's sole job is to protect your skin from UVA and UVB rays. You're in the sun every day if you live on earth in a place with windows. Wear. Your. SPF.

I don't believe in many absolute rules, but good SPF products are an absolute must.

Serum is usually a clear or clear-ish concentrated product that is lighter than and applied before moisturizer. Depending on how concentrated the product is (which will be stated on the packaging), you either rub it into your skin similar to a moisturizer or pat it into your skin. Serum contains concentrated ingredients like vitamin C, retinol, and hyaluronic acid that help your skin become smoother, more hydrated, and moisturized. When this is coupled with your moisturizer (which you put on after the serum), it typically makes a noticeable positive difference in your skin. While you can use serum during the day, using it at night is very effective because when you sleep your skin cells turn over and produce new cells to renew and repair your skin. This is one of the many reasons why a good night's rest is vital. Not only does your body rest, but your skin literally regenerates.

If we're being honest, the way you look often determines the way you feel. It's fine to implement healthy routines and processes that help you achieve how you want to look so you feel more confident in your day-to-day. Being aesthetically pleasing to yourself matters in a deep and meaningful way. It directly impacts your confidence. Your skin-care process doesn't have to be elaborate or include expensive products. It's all about taking care of your skin consistently and intentionally with what works for you.

EXERCISE

When it comes to working out, I love the results more than I hate the process. It's not my favorite, but exercising at least three to five times a week is one of those health goals I try to achieve.

MAGIC BUT REAL

Fitness doesn't come to me naturally. I don't like working out. But I always feel so good afterward. And I have more energy, feel strong, and look good in my clothes when I exercise on a consistent basis. So, no, I don't like the process of working out, but I really like the results. That's why I do it.

Right now, I'm in a season where I really enjoy walking. Especially in those weeks when it's transitioning from summer to fall and the mornings are bright yet cool, I love getting in outdoor walks. I have a track near my house that is half a mile one time around, so my goal is to do four laps in an hour. It usually helps me hit ten thousand steps for the day and gets my energy up quickly. I've been going so consistently lately that I can even jog nonstop for a mile. I normally go to the track three or four days out of the week in addition to some at-home workouts. Consistency pays off.

Because working out isn't something I love, having goals associated with it creates something to work toward, which matters to me.

My body always responds well to cardio. If I can't walk or run because of the weather or my schedule, we have an exercise bike with some great workout options. It's important to pay attention to not only what you like, but also what your body positively responds to. I've always been naturally lean and petite, but after having kids and as I've gotten older, I've found that burning fat requires much more effort. Keeping cardio consistently in my routine keeps my belly fat down and helps me to stay energetic throughout the day.

Even though I love cardio, it's important to me to strength train and have muscle. I really like feeling strong, and incorporating some sort of strength or weight training into my workouts has helped me to build muscle. I'll pull up a HIIT (high-intensity interval training), resistance, or kettlebell workout on YouTube and have at it for anywhere from fifteen to thirty minutes. That time works best for me.

Doing this regularly along with cardio is something I can enthusiastically commit to, and it gives me results I'm excited about.

You don't have to be a fitness expert or even "good" at working out to do it on a consistent basis. I certainly am not. Your commitment will get you further than your skill set will. For some people, having a personal trainer is what keeps them committed. For others, swimming laps is it. Listen, on those days I'm traveling and can't get in the gym, I will dance to my Beyoncé playlist for thirty minutes to burn those calories.

Staying physically active is a daily goal for me because it gives me energy, makes me feel strong, and helps me look good.

MAGIC MEMO

Start where you're at. Maybe you're lucky enough to live in a walkable neighborhood, have a gym at your workplace, or enjoy playing basketball at your local YMCA. Identify what physical activity challenges you yet makes you feel energetic and good afterward. Lean into it and commit to doing it at least one to three times a week. Increase the frequency after you get the hang of that rhythm after a few weeks if it works for you. There's also an array of online workout options—for free—to choose from if you feel like you don't have a lot of in-person options near you.

EATING WELL

"I haven't really eaten anything today." We've all been there. And it's nothing to brag about. Eating is important. Eating for energy is my priority. Truthfully, living in the United States can make you very jaded about food because we have so many choices and options. Admittedly, I am the take-out food queen, but if you want to eat healthy food that boosts your energy instead of depleting it, you're usually better off preparing it yourself.

If you're not into cooking, that's fine. It's still important to have the skills to make the most basic of meals, especially the kinds that nourish and energize your body.

Eating fruits and vegetables is important. My goal is to get four to five servings of fruits and vegetables on a daily basis. What makes an even bigger difference is eating produce that's in season.

To be clear, I love carbs, fried foods, ice cream, and wine. However, I don't like how they make me feel when I overindulge. As far as healthy, eat-for-energy foods, I like spinach, pico de gallo, ground turkey, brown rice, oatmeal, and zoodles (even though I reeeeeeeally HEART pasta). My goal with food is to enjoy what I eat because it gives me energy first, and then because it tastes good. I'll never give up carbs, but I'm happy and willing to enjoy them within reason.

FAITH

In 2011, I was pregnant for a short time before having a miscarriage. It was very traumatizing and truly shook me and Chris to the core.

When we visited the doctor afterward, he explained that I would likely never stay pregnant because of three large fibroid tumors, with the largest one being 9 cm (the size of a grapefruit). I remember praying so hard not only for the fibroids to go away without any invasive surgery, but also to have babies one day. This doctor basically told me that I wouldn't be able to have a successful pregnancy and even suggested that I have a hysterectomy. I was twenty-seven.

Luckily, I got a second and a third opinion, and they were a little different. But throughout that process, I prayed so hard my head would sometimes hurt. I just knew I would be able to get pregnant and have a baby because when I would pray, God told me I would.

It took almost three years, but I finally did get pregnant and delivered our first child, Maizah. It was a healthy pregnancy even with the fibroids. It got a little uncomfortable in the third trimester because of what they call fibroid degeneration. Basically, Maizah cut off the blood supply of the largest fibroid so it stopped growing.

An answered prayer. But it didn't stop there.

When I got pregnant with our second child, Caliana, I was concerned about the fibroid degeneration. They said it might happen, but the doctor wanted to just wait and see what the situation was when we got to the third trimester. On the day of my ultrasound during my final three months, everything looked great (we heard the baby's heartbeat and my vitals were fine), but the nurse looked stunned for some reason.

"Is everything okay?"

"I think so," she mumbled, still obviously surprised by something.

"Well, what is it?" I said impatiently.

"Your fibroid ... It's gone," she finally admitted. "In my eighteen years of doing this, I have never seen a fibroid just vanish. It's not behind the baby. It didn't even shrink. It's just...gone."

Another answered prayer. But there's more.

By the time I was pregnant with our son, Christian (our third child), the fibroids were pretty much nonexistent. When I was no longer pregnant, I didn't have painful or heavy periods like I did when I had fibroids. A decade before, a doctor looked me in the eye and told me to have my uterus removed because I wouldn't be able to carry a baby full-term, that I would never have a child.

Three kids later and God still has the last word in my life.

I love Jesus more than anything. Let's start there. He's done more for me than you'll ever know. As I grow in my faith, I pray throughout the day and read or listen to the Word consistently. Hearing is believing, and if I want to hear from God every day (which I do), I need to listen to His Word every day. I grew up Christian because my parents are believers, and we attended church as a family regularly throughout my life.

One day, at Bible study with my mom, the Word convicted me. I couldn't even tell you what it was, but after all the Sunday school stories, after all the memorizing of Bible verses and the so-called "right" Christian things to do, I just knew that Jesus was real. I could feel His presence in every single thing at that moment. From the smiles on people's faces to every shade of green of the leaves on the trees. On Wednesday, November 17, 1993, I answered the altar call and accepted Jesus as my Lord and Savior. The reason I remember this day so vividly is that I chose Him, on my own, without any prompting from a parent or adult. I was nine years old. It was the most important decision I've ever made for myself in my life.

My favorite thing about being a Christian is that I am not required to be perfect. If I were, I would've been kicked out of the club a long time ago. I try my best to extend grace and treat others the way I would like to be treated because of Him, not them. I miss the mark more often than I'd like to admit, but I thank God for the blood. As T. D. Jakes says, "The blood is the gospel."

Every morning I read the *Jesus Calling* devotional by Sarah Young and the verse of the day from the Holy Bible app. I pray with Chris, with the kids, and alone on a daily basis. As I continue to grow in my faith, I hear Him when He speaks and guides and I always pray that I will remain extra sensitive to the Holy Spirit. I don't want to miss anything He has for me. I try to make decisions that honor the kingdom first and foremost versus any approval from man. His love consumes me in a way that makes me realize the only thing I can do to come close to reciprocating that love is to live my life for Him.

Spending time with Him in prayer and listening to the Word are part of my spiritual health and self-care plan. Prayer re-centers me spiritually and reassures me that I am enough. Prayer is comforting. And prayer doesn't have to be an overly formal ritual, just personal and consistent. I pray in the shower, in the car, in the morning, at night, alone, and with others. Talking to Him has no boundaries in my life.

Whatever approach you take with your spiritual health, be intentional about it. Prayer, meditation, studying your beliefs, and taking time out to be still will do more for you than you'll ever expect. When you take care of your spirit and prioritize its health, I truly believe every other area of your health benefits.

If you know nothing else about me by the end of this book, know this: I am intentionally not everything to everyone because I don't have to be. He is my Everything. And that gives me the most peace.

MAGIC BUT REAL

I love Jesus, but I drink wine and cuss sometimes. Just want to be clear that my Christianity is not synonymous with perfection.

THERAPY

One day, after years of sweeping our issues under the rug and bouts of deep depression, Chris and I separated. However, we still spoke because we'd had our first child, and at one point he sent me a link from *Psychology Today*. It was contact information for a therapist.

It was the same therapist I continue to see today. I go consistently, at intervals ranging from once a month to once a week depending on my mental health needs.

I used to go to therapy to figure out what wasn't working for me. Now, I go to learn what's working and why so I can lean into it. Yes, God is my Everything. He also created therapy, and I'm happy to use what He created.

What I love about therapy are the epiphanies I have once I dissect an experience, thought, or concern of mine. I love that it's both deep and basic—the revelations are often elementary and simple once realized, which is incredibly freeing.

Therapy is all about learning about yourself. Think about it—as an adult, where else do you get to work on yourself without the process relating to anyone else? Sure, life (and work for that matter) is all about relationships, but if you can't get a handle on the relationship with yourself, how will you be able to successfully function in any other one? We often are reacting and responding to others, but when do we get to decide and decipher how we feel and how we've grown?

This is exactly the sort of space that therapy provides. If you've been considering therapy, I feel certain that you can benefit from it when you find the right therapist. And I will say, therapists aren't like hairstylists, in that you should share them with friends or family members. Go out of your way to find someone who's right for you with no bias or connection to anyone who has a bias toward you to ensure it's a right fit. Going to therapy doesn't mean that anything is wrong with you. It's just that you're willing to go a step further to do the work of knowing and understanding yourself. It's a good decision.

Let's stop making good decisions a chore. They're a choice. Therapy is your choice. Do not let anyone make you feel bad for making a choice to take care of yourself.

Attaining health through self-care is deep work, deliberate work, and disciplined work that is always worth it. It looks different for all of us. It also looks different through the different seasons of your life. It takes time and you should always remind yourself that you're worth taking time for. You're worth being disciplined for. You're worth taking care of. You may be using self-care as a break and using it only in case of emergency when you should actually use it as an update of your "self-software." Stay up-to-date on caring for yourself. Stop using self-care as the last straw.

Making your health MAGIC means making your self-care meaningful (not just aimlessly indulgent) with necessary appointments, making yourself aesthetically pleasing in your eyes with your physical health and skin care, setting goals that encourage you to exercise and eat for energy, intentionally prioritizing your faith and beliefs, and consistently improving your mental health with therapy and "you days."

CHAPTER THREE

Making Your Space MAGIC

Clear space, clear mind.

When I was growing up, we lived in a gorgeous home outside of Pittsburgh. It was the largest home we'd ever lived in and my mom was (and still is) quite the homemaker. Like me, she liked nice things (the apple doesn't fall far from the tree) and believed in a place for everything. She also believed in seeing the vacuum tracks in the carpet. From time to time, my sister and I would walk through the formal living room that no one was allowed in because that's where all the nice furniture and items in our house were located. When Mom would ask us if we walked through the living room, we'd try to get away with a little white lie and say no but she always knew. You know why? She would see our footprints in her freshly vacuumed living room carpet. She always knew.

Now, I'm not partial to vacuum tracks in my living room carpet—the kids can walk freely in our living room. However, I have to admit that I have become my mom. I cannot take it when the kids run in the formal dining room, which is where a lot of our "nice things" are. I have a little more patience with them than my mom did with us, but after asking them to get out for the third time, it may or may not turn into yelling. I'm one of those people who have a table setting on the formal dining room table throughout the year—one for the spring and summer, one for the fall, one for the holidays, and another for winter. Then I rinse and repeat when spring rolls around.

What can I say? I take home decor seriously. Don't worry, this isn't the chapter where I tell you how you should decorate your house to look like something on Pinterest. But we are going to talk about the things in your home—be it an apartment, house, condo, et cetera—and how to keep them in order and make your space MAGIC.

I like "stuff." I'm a materialistic person who likes her things. Somewhere along the line someone lied to us and told us liking things was bad. I understand that things are not more important than people and that having certain things doesn't make you better than anyone else. That said, having things is not bad. In fact, having the right stuff can improve a situation. On the other hand, material objects can have a negative effect if you're not careful. You can absolutely overdose on things. Things can cause you to be overwhelmed, confused, and even delusional when you don't manage them responsibly.

God created things for us to enjoy—so enjoy them. But we cannot get to a place where we start to worship them or care about them more than people or even ourselves. And if you're blessed to have things you like and appreciate, keeping them in order and in their place is your responsibility. Again, this doesn't mean that you have to become obsessive about cleaning or even organize to the level of a professional organizer. Having a place for all your things is necessary and has to be done intentionally. Whether or not you consider yourself organized has nothing to do with it. If you have things, you have to find a place for them and figure out a process to maintain that organization that works for you. Open space isn't enough of a place; the place for your things has to have noticeable function, sometimes visibility, and always purpose.

As much as I like things, I cannot deal with them all over the place, and I don't like when everyone in my family asks me where everything is.

When stuff is all over the place, I've found that I (along with my family) don't appreciate it as much and can sometimes mistreat it. Even worse, it's possible to forget that you have certain things and end up buying them again. I know this from experience. Not only is this a misuse of your time, but it's abusive to your resources and proves that you lack order. There's no magic in lacking order. This is why I fully believe in having a place for everything because you literally create peace of mind when you do.

When we have too much stuff or don't have a designated place for our things, this causes clutter. Clutter is a mess and mess equals stress. This isn't just my opinion. According to studies, cortisol (the stress hormone) is noticeably higher in mothers who live in a cluttered household. Clutter can cause anxiety, reduce our working memory, and trigger unhealthy eating habits. When a room is cluttered, we're more likely to reach for chocolate than an apple. Clutter is a visual distraction that literally causes us to make decisions that hurt us more than help us. When you make better decisions at home, you make better decisions in life.

When you decide where your things go and create routines to ensure that they are consistently put in place, you're showing yourself and God that you appreciate the things you have and are willing to do the work to take care of them. To find a place for everything, you need to make meaningful decisions regarding where they belong. The MAGIC of things isn't the thing itself, it's how you manage, appreciate, and place it.

We all have things, and the goal with things is to enjoy them and give them direction so they provide usefulness at home. To manage means "to be in charge of or to run something." So ask yourself: Do I manage the things in my home in an efficient manner? Dishes, clothes, toys, furniture, mail, books—Are you in charge of your things or are your things in charge of you? As optimistic as I am, it's impossible to make everyday MAGIC in household clutter. Your goal is to get your home in order, to always be aware of all things in your home and how they make it better. Doing regular inventory—on a monthly and quarterly basis—and prioritizing "things planning" will help you manage your things efficiently.

To effectively manage the things in your space, you have to remember why the space matters to you in the first place.

Why does the kitchen matter in your space?

Why does your living room matter to your family?

Why does your bedroom matter to you?

Sure, it's easy to answer these questions from a technical point of view—the kitchen is where you prepare food, the living room is where you spend family time, and your bedroom is where you sleep. But that is simply the function of your space. Why does a particular room matter to you?

In our home, the kitchen is typically where my family takes their vitamins before starting their day and where the kids dump their bookbags and lunch boxes after school. In the evenings, it's where I prepare for the next day, whether it's writing in my planner or making school lunches. Sometimes Chris and I make decisions and have family-focused discussions in the kitchen after the kids are asleep. It's also where family and friends congregate for conversation if they're over for the holidays or a special occasion. Essentially, it's the nucleus of our home. So making it feel and look welcoming—to my family as well as visitors—is essential. It's the reason why I keep the kitchen island clear at the end of the day, so it feels open to having important conversations. When the kitchen counters are clear, I'm more focused on writing notes in my planner for the next day.

Understanding why your space matters to you and your family allows you to make more meaningful decisions about how you want it to look and where certain items in it should be placed. This looks different for all of us because certain spaces mean different things to all of us.

It's impossible to manage what doesn't matter and so if you find that a certain space in your home is always cluttered, step back and ask yourself why that matters to you. If it doesn't matter, what could you do with the space to make it matter to you?

NICE THINGS

Growing up I remember my mom saying something along the lines of, "Let's save that nice thing for something special." In fact, she still says it when I wear something "nice" just because, and I always tell her, "Everyday life deserves nice things too." Life is short, and even if we are in fact saving the nice thing for something special, I'm something special—am I not? I remember how growing up we would save nice dishes for when company came over and wear nice clothes to only fancy occasions or venues. In hindsight, we ended up not wearing a lot of those nice things or using those nice dishes very often. I like nice things—I am materialistic and I know it—but I like using the nice things I have. Nice things have a purpose and they shouldn't be saved for only when a big or special moment happens. And nice things aren't exclusively things that you must buy.

What is a nice thing? My definition of a nice thing is an object or experience of value or attractiveness to you. That means a nice thing is something that you deem useful (value) and that is appealing to your senses (attractiveness). This meaning is unique to every single person because we all have different preferences and value different things. What may be a nice thing to you may not be a nice thing to me and vice versa. What should be understood even further is that the fact that I don't view the thing as nice doesn't mean it should matter any less to you. Your nice things simply matter to you most.

Every day deserves nice things simply because. Every day we wake up and do the work to be our best selves, take care of our family, contribute to our home, and design a life that matters to us. That's a lot of work. When you add up all you do every day, nice things are a little sprinkle of grace you very likely can use. My favorite thing about normalizing nice things for myself is that when it's time to do something nice for someone else, I have a solid arsenal to pull from since it's the default of my everyday life.

I believe nice things can be seen, heard, and felt, and even if it's in the littlest way, incorporating something nice into your everyday life is a guaranteed way to look forward to it. This isn't about something necessarily being expensive or even fancy, but it's okay if it is. Overall, it's about the nice things elevating the MAGIC in your life. We discussed this earlier: Beautiful things (again, what you deem beautiful) make you feel beautiful. So the more you can surround yourself with beautiful sounds, sights, and sensations, the nicer every day will be. Here's what's also true: Even with everyday MAGIC, there will always be hard days and some days where you just can't get out of the starting blocks right. This is why normalizing nice things every day is so important. It's not just to be frivolous and materialistic; it often turns out to be your saving grace on the days you need it most.

Stop saving nice things for a time when something special

happens, or for when you travel or when you have family and friends over. You're something special, so is your space, and you deserve nice things every day.

Going outside is a nice thing I try to give myself every day. Nothing beats sunlight—aka God's ring light. It is unmatched. No matter the season, the sun hitting your face isn't just a nice thing, it's a blessing. And they say that if you can see it, you can be it. My mother-in-law once told me, "You should always aim to be the light, even in dark places. Especially there." On those really stressful or emotionally draining days, stepping outside is a serious game changer. Whether you work from home (especially if you work from home) or at your workplace, normalize walking outdoors even for ten minutes a day. This is a nice thing that can't be bought and certainly not replaced. It's self-care, a nice thing, and exercise all tied up in one bundle.

If you follow me on Instagram, you know that I order fresh flowers for my home every other week. It's something I look forward to and it really elevates my mood and the entire mood of the house. The kids even comment on it and share how much they like it. Hubs will even chime in and say how good the formal dining room looks when you walk in. Flowers are one of those nice things that never get old in my opinion. They're always so beautiful to look at. I get four arrangements—one for the kitchen, two for the formal dining room, and one for the master bathroom. I can't explain it but having fresh flowers in the master bathroom just makes me feel so luxe and worthy. The best part is that flowers are nice whether they're from the florist or Trader Joe's. Thirty dollars' worth of flowers from the grocery store could be the nice thing you've been needing after some stressful days at work. Get a vase or a mason jar, put your favorite flowers together in a beautiful arrangement, and set them on your bathroom counter. Simply the sight of them as you walk into your bathroom the next morning will elevate the start of your day. If you take just a handful of advice from this book, let this be part of it. Buy yourself fresh flowers and put some in your bathroom. You'll be so glad you did.

Are fresh flowers really worth the hassle? According to studies, yes. Not only do fresh flowers give you a burst of positive energy, but they also encourage creativity. Whenever I have fresh flowers around, my mood is brighter, as is the mood of anyone who's in the same room. The vibe of the room where I have fresh flowers is light and calm—like a literal breath of fresh air. If the flowers have a scent—like lavender—it can help reduce stress, anxiety, and pain while also helping you sleep better. The long and the short of it is that seeing fresh flowers in your space helps you unwind. Because intentionally making sure you have aesthetically pleasing—aka nice—things in your space is a way of designing your environment. Studies show that environmental design greatly impacts your mental and physical health.

Good music is always nice to hear, and you should listen to some good music every day. Listening to your favorite artist or album can bring up some great memories where you reminisce about growing up or a special moment in your life. I think we all can agree that music is powerful. It can change your bad mood to a good one in a matter of seconds. It can take a boring moment and make it lively in minutes. It can take you from dragging during a workout to powering through like a champ. Music is meaningful, that's what makes it MAGIC.

Don't underestimate listening to music throughout your day when you can and be careful of what you're listening to. I have moments when I'm listening to popular or party music that has lyrics I wouldn't play in front of my kids. I'm grown and there's nothing wrong with that. But sometimes love songs, praise songs, or songs from my favorite musical can be the nice thing that keeps my everyday afloat.

Do not underestimate the power of a great playlist. Create different playlists for different moods or types of days you may be having. Creating the playlists in advance takes time, but it's time well spent. Intentionally listening to nice things elevates your brain health. According to studies by Johns Hopkins University, listening to music keeps your brain young; in a way, listening to music gives your brain a workout. Not only that, it can also help reduce anxiety and blood pressure in addition to improving things like the quality of your sleep, mood, and memory.

It's also nice to hear soothing sounds.

Since the kids were babies, we've always played white noise to help them go to sleep, and now they all sleep to sounds of the ocean we found on Spotify. Those wave sounds are so soothing that once we put them on, it's hard for them to not fall into a peaceful sleep. Chris and I also listen to a deep sleep music mix and have our Google Home play it when we go to bed. I'm not sure what it is, but whenever we play it I fall asleep so deeply and peacefully. It's one of those nice things I don't take for granted because it makes a big difference in how I go to sleep and wake up the next morning. If I'm not feeling the deep sleep mix, I'll play nature sounds from a meditation app like sounds of the lake or beach to fall asleep to. Sounds of water are soothing to me; they especially help me when I've had a really stressful day. Everyone has a sound that helps them relax, calm down, or even focus. Your nice thing might be sounds of the rain forest as you get some work done. It's about finding what works for you and using it to your advantage every day. Simple, soothing sounds can be powerful as your nice thing to hear.

One thing that I think we all deserve is hearing nice things from ourselves—aka affirmations. There's something about saying our affirmations that makes them more true than just reading them silently or saying them in our heads. Hearing is believing, and we want to believe ourselves when we speak life into ourselves. This seems silly at first, but after you do it consistently, you'll realize how much power it has. The two affirmations I tell myself every day are "I love you" and "I'm proud of you." I say these while looking at myself in the mirror. This is another way to see a nice thing, and it really goes a long way. It doesn't have to be long and drawn out, but look yourself in the eyes and mean what you say. If you can't say what you mean to yourself, how will you be able to say it to others?

Hear yourself say nice things about yourself like:

"My body is beautiful."

"I am beautiful."

"I'm reliable."

"I love myself."

"I'm proud of myself."

"I believe in myself and my abilities."

"I trust myself."

"I let go of my fears."

"I have all that it takes to be successful and confident."

"I choose wisely and carefully."

Hearing positive affirmations reiterates them as truth now rooted in self-perception, which makes them believable and your new default. This is one of the nicest things you can do for yourself. Doing it every day and making it a habit isn't just MAGIC, it's deliberate self-care.

We discussed that self-care isn't solely about indulging; however, indulging in feeling nice things is good. Wearing luxurious fabrics and beautiful clothing that feels good is self-care. I love wearing dresses and getting dolled up, but one of the nicest things I've worn and felt comfortable in is a plain white T-shirt. There are these five-dollar T-shirts from Target that are so comfy and go with anything—they are hands down one of my favorite things. They're made out of cotton that feels better next to my skin than almost any other fabric in my closet. They're soft yet durable and complement a skirt as well as they do a pair of jeans. Then I have these silk pajamas that remind me just how important good pajamas are. When you put them on, it's like wearing a soft, luxurious hug. You feel luxe, you feel good, and you're certainly comfortable enough to easily fall asleep. They're pricey, but sometimes nice things are expensive.

You and your space deserve nice things every day—whether they're free, affordable, or expensive. It's a way to take care of yourself and improve your health. Make space for nice things every day to extend grace to yourself and allow yourself to indulge.

STORING YOUR THINGS

There are things in all our homes that need to be managed on a consistent basis to avoid clutter—paper, clothing, food, containers, supplies, appliances, and miscellaneous items. The goal should be to find a place for everything that matters in your space.

To keep paper clutter to a minimum, having a binder system has helped me tremendously. The truth is when you become an adult, paper will follow you. (Yep, even in a technologically advanced world.) There's the warranties, doctor's records, notarized documents, and other papers that need to be kept for future reference in all of our lives. It's expensive and inconvenient to have them replaced, so keeping them in a safe place is a must. Binders with plastic sheet protectors have been a godsend for me over the last few years.

The binders that I keep on a shelf in our home office include:

Car documents
House documents
Kids' artwork
School documents
Medical records
Manuals and warranties

Using accessories like tab dividers to organize the content within the binders and printing spine and front covers help to identify which binders are which. For paper mail, I have a pretty wire bin by the front door where it's easily stored. Once it's full, we go through it and toss what's no longer needed. In most cases, we toss 95 percent of it. The rest can usually go to its appropriate home office binder.

If you don't have that many documents, keeping a file box, file organizer, or fireproof document storage bag is a great option as well. For a family of five with a lot of stuff, having a binder system makes the most sense for our home.

I keep personal documents that need to be protected at all times, like birth certificates, passports, and Social Security cards, in a fire-proof box.

While we'll discuss clothing when we talk about the MAGIC of things in a later chapter, the general rule in our home is that everyone has velvet space-saving hangers in their closets. Chris and I use black, and the kids use pink, lavender, and gray. The hangers allow us to maximize space in our closets while protecting our clothes (the velvet is gentle on almost all fabrics). We also provide velvet hangers in the guest room.

For the clothing items that can't be hung, we file-fold them and place them in drawers and include drawer separators in some cases as well. I know that's not how you and I were likely taught growing up and it takes a little extra time, but it's worth it. File-folding saves you time because you can actually see what's in your drawers since the "filed" clothes are standing up, not stacked. Also, you end up having more space for more clothes. You can thank Marie Kondo for that.

MAGIC BUT REAL

There are days when I don't feel like getting my Marie Kondo on and file-folding something. I'll throw it in a drawer and deal with it later. You know why? Because I'm tired. And if the drawer can close, no one can see it and the closet or room still appears clean. Magic.

Placing things is both an aesthetically pleasing and intentional part of making your space MAGIC. Not sure if you're like me, but I truly committed to the KonMari method when Marie Kondo blessed us with the question "Does it spark joy?" I happily binge-watched her Netflix show and eagerly watched people's lives be transformed because they decided to get rid of the things that didn't spark their joy and contribute to their everyday MAGIC. Placing things happens whether you're intentional or not. When you're intentional about where you place things, though, you're positioning the things for usefulness. When you're not intentional, you're positioning the things to be useless and to be added to clutter. Intentionality requires you to be thoughtful, not just indulgent; it requires a relevant honesty that must be coupled with active decisiveness. How you place things determines whether or not you will be able to find them and utilize them when necessary.

Ask yourself, Do I keep my things in order? When things are out of order, they don't work. Think about it—when you see the "Out of Order" sign on a bathroom stall, what does that tell you? It doesn't work. This also applies to our stuff. Sometimes we might think that a thing doesn't work for our lives because it's out of order when the case might be that it's simply misplaced. Only keeping things in order will tell you whether or not something does have value (aka usefulness) in your life.

When it comes to storing food in the pantry, I am adamant about using containers to help keep snacks, ingredients, and canned goods organized so they're easy to find come mealtime. As someone who didn't have a pantry for ten years of our marriage, I can say that organizing your cabinets, cupboards, and drawers will be incredibly helpful as well. I'm all about storing like with like. So all of our chips are in the chip bin—a large plastic bin where I file all of our chips or chip-like snacks. I reclose the bags with color-coded clips. All of the kids' snacks for school and after school are color-coded in clear containers on one shelf. Clear containers are great because they help you eliminate confusion and the need to rummage through a bin or container to find what you're looking for.

I keep like with like in kitchen cabinets as well. I keep all the plastic lids filed in a bin to the right of where I have all their matching plastic containers. We had so many of them and they were always hard to organize until one day I bought all the same kind. I have square, rectangular, and circle-shaped containers. For each shape, I bought three sizes—small, medium, and large. This makes storing them simple because within each group, they all perfectly stack into or on top of one another. They're super-affordable black containers with clear lids that I believe we got from a dollar store or Amazon. It's not about being fancy as much as being functional. Function = MAGIC.

In the garage, you guessed it, we keep like with like as far as storage is concerned. Clear oversized bins and shelving are your best friends in the garage, so you can easily see where items are and give yourself more storage space. When you can see your things and easily access them, you increase the likelihood of your appreciating them.

MAGIC MEMO

Buy a lot of the same containers. Same color and same size, depending on what you're using them for. This is just a wonderful hack for making things look seamless and organized even if you're naturally not. If it's for the kids, I'll usually buy the same containers for each of them in different colors, so everyone has their own bin. For baking goods, I use medium-sized bins all across one shelf of my pantry. For flour and sugar, I use the same large glass jars. Sameness creates visual order in spaces. And the containers don't have to be fancy, just functional. You can get them from anywhere including Amazon, the Container Store, Walmart, or Target depending on your preference or budget.

GET IT DONE

If there is no place for a thing in your home, this is also when you decide if something needs to be purged—or placed somewhere else. The goal with your space should be to keep things that matter and purge the rest. When you no longer have a use for certain things—baby items, appliances, and the like—you have three purge options: you can toss, gift, or donate. I like to purge on designated Get It Done days. A Get It Done day is when you designate a day in the month or quarter to place or purge your things for a certain room in your home. Some Get It Done days are for the garage, others are for your closet, like we will discuss in chapter 7. The whole purpose of Get It Done days is just that: to get it done. Not some of it, *all* of it. Decide ahead of time what day you're going to Get It Done (Saturday or Sunday usually works best for me) and determine what tools or items you'll need. Having at least a fourteen- to thirty-day lead time is realistic because you won't forget about it and that gives you time to prepare for the day thoroughly. Anything shorter and you're rushing and then stress is inevitable. Anything further out becomes forgettable. Ask for help or hire it out since you have the time. When you schedule your Get It Done day, start early, commit to it even when it becomes harder than you thought it would be, and, most importantly, finish.

You'll likely need only two to four Get It Done days in the year. You don't need to make them any more frequent than that because you want to actually enjoy your life. And the goal here is to put things in their place and create order, not to become obsessive.

Toss out anything that is broken, expired, outdated, soiled, or beyond repair. Give away things to your close friends or family (aka your village), or to someone who could use what you have in the current season of their life. Text them immediately and see if they would like to have it. If they say yes, make specific arrangements to get it to them ASAP. (The goal is to purge things and get them out of your home fast.) If they say no, donate it. Anything that doesn't need to be tossed and can't be given to anyone in your close friend and family circle should be donated. Decide ahead on the organization you want to donate to—I like to choose local and small nonprofit organizations who will really value the items. Then coordinate and schedule pickup or drop-off.

Consistently appreciating your space and the things in it is part of your everyday MAGIC. Appreciating your things is all about actually using them. But here's the thing about using what you have: you have to be present to remember to use it. How present are you when you're at home? Are you on the move, just preparing to go to work or school the next day? Are you scrolling on your phone the whole time and act like your family is interrupting you when they ask for your attention? Do you actually like the place you call home? Once upon a time I didn't like our home, and so I would buy stuff all the time or go out all the time to avoid being home. The problem wasn't my home itself, it was my appreciation of it. I didn't think the things I had were enough, so I didn't take care of them or organize them in a way that encouraged me to use them. And guess what would happen? When friends and family came over, they would say things like: "I didn't know you had this!" or "You have some great things!" and that started to change my perspective.

You are overwhelmingly blessed even if you consider what you have little. However, your nonstop scrolling on social media has made you addicted to comparing yourself and what you have to strangers and what you think they have. Please don't value smoke and mirrors over the actual goodness that's right in front of you. You likely have more than you think, but you're not present enough to even realize your blessing. Put the phone down, take a good look at your things—yes, the material things—and remember the time you used to pray to have something like them. Your bed, your apartment, your garage, your pantry, your walk-in closet, those bins your mom bought you from Amazon, your favorite house slippers, your perfume, and so on. These are all things I want you to see and use and revel in, because I guarantee you that having these things wasn't always the default for you. It certainly wasn't for me. They say, "Stop and smell the roses," and your home, no matter where you live, is "the roses." Use what you have, take care of your things, and, most importantly, appreciate them.

Having a Pinterest-worthy home isn't what makes your space valuable; how you take care of it makes it valuable to you. That has nothing to do with being the perfect organizer or keeping your home unrealistically tidy. It is about order and how that order helps you appreciate the things you have and the home you live in. Sure, it takes extra time to file-fold, and you and I both know you could use some containers in the pantry to get the snacks in order for your family. Remember that getting your space and its things in order adds a peace to your home that's unmatched and certainly worth the effort. If you're looking to elevate the vibe of your space almost instantly, normalizing nice things and finding a place for everything (and purging when necessary) will certainly do that.

CHAPTER FOUR

The MAGIC of Family

Family matters.

When I was growing up, my disciplinarian West African father was adamant about his children not watching TV on weekdays. However, when the weekend hit, he and Mommy were great at making sure we had fun. They'd take us to the playground, and we'd go to Blockbuster on Friday nights to rent a couple of movies and Mommy would make these delicious shortbread biscuits with strawberries and whipped cream that we always ate during the movie. The biscuits weren't anything fancy, but they were delicious. Those weekends were some of my first experiences with family traditions.

I really love having a family. Being a mom is a *lot* of work. Confession: I'm not a kid person, or even a patient one at that. My best friend is remarkable at being a mom. She's patient, kind, and sort of like the kid whisperer. It was a no-brainer to make her the godmother of our kids. Me? I lose patience when I have to repeat myself and often forget that I have been here on earth six times longer than my oldest child. I've read all the books, watched the IG live streams from parenting experts, and learned from those who are more patient than me. It just doesn't come naturally for me. Here's what I know: Being a "kid person" doesn't have to come naturally to me, and my parenting style doesn't have to look like someone else's. My job as a mom is to put forth the effort to be the best mom I can be every day. Some days are better than others. Physical touch doesn't matter to me (I'm much more a words of affirmation or acts of service kind of girl), but I know how important it is to be physically affectionate with my kids. So I give lots of hugs, and sure, all three of them can lean on me during screen time when all I actually want to do is watch TV—alone. It's fine. Being a mom isn't easy, but it's worth it. I truly do love being a mom even though I'm not perfect at it.

Here's what I am good at—making a moment. I love a spectacle, be it small or large, and making a spectacle for my family is something I want to make a norm. There are certain things that matter to each of our families that are worth making a big deal out of. We love watching movies, eating pancakes, and letting the sun hit our faces, so we've built family traditions around each of those things. Whether it's every week, every month, or even once a year, find those traditions that matter to your family. Find stuff your family *loves*. And then live what you love. It gives you something to look forward to and it's always worth it.

One of the most meaningful things you can do as a family is spend time together. We make time for all of us as a family, but it is just as important to make sure that as a couple Chris and I spend quality time together. While special occasions are a great time to go out and celebrate as a couple, I've learned that dating each other regularly, even just on a normal day, sets a healthy standard in a relationship.

I love dating my husband. He's a lot of fun to be around and gives me space to be fun as well. I like an elaborate date at a fancy museum or going to a concert as much as I like going to the movies to see the latest Marvel release. Intentionality and consistency always make date nights special, even when they're "just" going to the movies, because they give you something to look forward to as a couple. There are so many responsibilities that you often have to tackle as a duo—parenting, bills, housework, and the like—that it can become overwhelming if there is no balance of enjoying each other as well. When I talk to my friends who are married or in a relationship and they're at odds with their partners, I listen first and then I often ask, "When's the last time you guys went out, just the two of you?" Sometimes it's important to be selfish with your partner and have uninterrupted time with them outside of the house. Quality time, shared experiences, and intimate conversation are often the glue in a healthy relationship because they prioritize connection. I'm selfish when it comes to my husband—I want him all to myself on a regular basis, not just when it's one of our birthdays or another special occasion.

He's my favorite. So, I make a real effort to create space in our schedules to ensure that we have two to four date nights every month.

If you're married or have a partner, when do you make time for just the two of you?

When's the last time the two of you went out on a date?

Do you implement date night as a regular thing or only for special moments like birthdays and anniversaries?

If it's not already a consistent thing, how can you make date night more regular? What are some free or affordable ways to date each other?

MAGIC BUT REAL

Hubs tells the kids all the time that they're his second-favorite. He always goes, "I love you, but I love your mom more. If it wasn't for her, you wouldn't be here." It's become an inside joke with all of us, but I love that in jest and truth we've expressed to the kids that we truly love each other and put our marriage first. So when they see that "Mom and Dad are going out," while they stay with their grandparents or godparents, they understand that as much as we love them, we have to take time out for ourselves too.

I'm no marriage expert and will never attempt to be one because I'm too busy trying to make sure my marriage stays intact. Here's what I will say, though: never stop dating your spouse. If you've read books on having a successful marriage, you've likely run across that and it's true. Spending time with each other, not as parents and outside of your home, is vital to the heartbeat of your marriage. You never want it to feel stale and boring and to always feel that there is something to look forward to. Chris and I try our very best to schedule in a date once a week, but if we miss the mark we are adamant about not letting two weeks pass without being kid-free for a meal. Because we work together as well, I cannot stress enough how imperative this time is.

TRADITIONS AROUND FOOD

Hubs loves pancakes. He loves them so much that he has made all of us love pancakes too. So Saturday morning is reserved for pancakes made from scratch—à la Hubs—and a full-blown breakfast. We're a eat-dinner-at-the-table-every-day kind of family, but during the week the kids eat breakfast before hopping in the car for school, and sometimes when we're running late breakfast is eaten on-the-go in the car. On Saturdays, we're able to enjoy breakfast together.

My husband believes in making most things from scratch because he's a great cook. That's one of the perks of marrying a man from New Orleans: he can cook his face off. Pancakes are one of his specialties. But in addition to that, he also makes us breakfast potatoes, a spinach skillet, scrambled eggs, and bacon. (We get this delicious bacon that leaves you speechless from our local meat market.) We typically sleep in on Saturday mornings because, rest. But by 10:00 a.m., the house smells like breakfast glory. Good food produces good moods, and that's exactly what we're in when it's breakfast time on Saturday mornings.

During this time the kids help set the table and we really let them get hands-on since we're not on a grueling weekday schedule. Maizah and Caliana will help their dad with the pancake batter and Christian usually gets in a chair on his own and excitedly waits for food.

We go all out. I normally sous-chef, cutting up fruit to top the pancakes and setting the food on the table. We always, *always* listen to Afro-Cuban or New Orleans funk radio on Pandora on Saturday mornings. It's a tradition that came from nowhere it seems, but it's just what we do on Saturdays, my friends. The kids are as invested as we are and that's what makes it wonderful.

MAGIC MEMO

Select your home/family soundtrack. I believe that every home should have a soundtrack because it creates the mood for your family togetherness. On Saturdays, it's New Orleans funk or Afro-Cuban all-stars. If our house could listen to only one album all day long, it would be Stevie Wonder's *Songs in the Key of Life*. Now, whenever the kids hear Stevie Wonder, they'll think of home.

What does your family love to eat?
What kind of music makes you all feel good?
Does your family have a Saturday morning tradition?

If you don't, what might be a good tradition to start on Saturday mornings?

"What's for dinner?" is the question that can wipe me out completely no matter how good things are going in my life. Something deep inside of me is always like, "AGAIN?!" and the answer is always, "Yes, again." We have to eat every day, and what a blessing it is to have the means to buy food, with many options to choose from, as well as clean water to drink. It has become this daunting first world "problem" that we internally overcomplicate. Making dinner feels more daunting than preparing the other meals—breakfast seems simple enough and even lunch feels like a curious yet welcomingly anticipated puzzle to solve. But when I'm done with my workday, having decided what to eat for the first two meals, and I don't have the answer to "What's for dinner?" I want to scream.

This is why I almost always decide what's for dinner ahead of time. Mealtime matters—not just dinner, but all of them—and thinking about a meal ahead of time is worthwhile. You *can* make healthier decisions and not rely on takeout every night of the week; plus, planning gives you the power to set the mood for what you want to eat. It's a small yet simple way to get everyone in the family—yourself included—excited and looking forward to the next meal, whether it's breakfast in the morning, lunch at school tomorrow, or dinner in an hour.

Meal planning has become a sensation over the last few years. A quick Google search warrants about 398 million results in less than a second. If that doesn't tell you we all have an issue with "What's for dinner?" I don't know what will. You don't have to be a gourmet chef or even a "good cook" to master the magic of mealtime. You just have to be clear on what you're trying to achieve and what resources you're going to need to achieve it.

I grocery shop every week—sometimes a couple of times a week depending on what's in stock and what we have planned for the week. If I need some ingredients fresher than a week old, I'll wait and order them a day or two ahead of time. But what I've learned to do so we don't have a bunch of food waste is to plan meals based on ingredients that we currently have and that are in season. And plan your meals ahead of time—even if just a couple of days ahead—so you can avoid decision burnout. I like to plan all my meals for the week ahead, then buy needed groceries based on the plan; and, because I have small children, I have to think about everyone's preferences and aversions. (We don't have any known allergies, but that's another thing to consider if it applies at your house.)

MAGIC MEMO

I try my best not to make the same meal on the same day every week. The exception to this rule in my household is Spaghetti Mondays; and at my best friend's house it's Taco Tuesdays. Again, traditions are great because they bring consistency to something you and your loved ones really enjoy. Not everyone enjoys the same food every single day of the week. You want to be thoughtfully consistent more than frequently monotonous when it comes to meals. It's all about balance—meals, even if consistent in ingredients or entrée, should feel refreshing when presented.

I'm all about cooking what we eat. If you have small kids, it's hard to try that new delicious lamb chop recipe you saw on Pinterest. Your kids may not like lamb chops, and it's expensive when you try new things and your kids don't eat them. Trying new things is important, though, and there's space for that when you go out to eat or even on the weekends. But when the kids have to get in bed for school in the morning, you want to ensure that their little bellies are full, so they don't wake up hungry asking for a snack. And also, you simply want them to be well nourished and satisfied.

For the most part, we all know what each member of our family likes to eat and what we need to eat to get our nutrients in. If it was up to my kids, we would eat bread, cheese, and fruit snacks all day, but that is certainly not worth it when no one can go to the bathroom for three days. I don't force my kids to eat brussels sprouts, but I always present colors on the plate to introduce them to whole foods (fruits and vegetables) and, most importantly, to normalize those choices. At our house, we eat a ton of fresh fruits every day. Apples, oranges, bananas, grapes, strawberries, cherries, kiwis, and more—honestly, it's tough to keep fruit in my house for more than seventy-two hours. That is one of our eating strengths for sure. All of us could stand to eat more vegetables so I try to keep green veggies around, with a sprinkle of other colors for good measure. We typically eat broccoli and green beans without fuss, but I try to incorporate other veggies like carrots, spinach, bell peppers, zucchini, squash, and more as well.

Aside from the nutrient-dense whole foods, I also make it my business to cook what we like to eat. We all eat chicken, fish, and turkey. Hubs and I like shrimp and beef, while the kids aren't huge fans.

The kids love some potatoes, rice, and pasta, but Hubs and I definitely can't digest the white processed foods like we used to. So if I'm making sides with potatoes or white rice for the kids, I'll swap it out with wild rice or sweet potatoes for the two of us. We love pasta, so I'll make different variations of that. Sometimes it's spaghetti (every Monday) with a meat sauce. Some Mondays it's ground turkey; other Mondays it's ground beef or even chicken. Other times I'll switch it up and make a penne pasta with salmon and Alfredo sauce and sneak in some veggies. The variety is nice while staying true to what we eat. If you're a sheet-pan cooking family, sheet-pan all the types of protein and veggies you like for different meal options. You guys live for breakfast? Make a big deal with omelets, waffles, or even pastries.

MAGIC MOMENT

"Can I help, Mom?" I love getting things done efficiently in my own way, so when the kids ask if they can help me in the kitchen, I have to catch myself and think about the bigger picture before immediately declining their offer. I love my kids. I also love to clean as I cook and bake to make cleaning go faster. When you cook or bake with kids, that's almost impossible. But guess what? Fast cleanup doesn't matter when you see those sweet faces excitedly rush to the kitchen and grab their aprons. Again, unless I'm in a hurry, when they ask, "Can I help?" I feel like it's my duty as Mom to willingly say yes. That yes not only answers their question in their favor, but it also validates their value in the kitchen and at home. That is a big deal. Everyone was a beginner, and we only get better and more experienced when someone says, "Yes, I'll show you how to do it, and you can give it a try." What better place to do that than at home.

My pound cake from scratch is my specialty and my oldest always wants to help when I bake it. There's something magical about being able to help make something you love. I feel that way when I bake myself and I imagine that's what it does for her. She's been attached to getting good at cracking eggs lately after watching baking videos on YouTube Kids. It's the part she always wants to do, and it secretly stresses me out. But I always remember that you have to start somewhere and I'm glad it's at home. Turns out, she's pretty good at it. Sure, there are some eggshell casualties that we have to clean out of the batter, but it's worth it when I hear her squeal to her dad that she helped me bake the cake.

Once you get clear on knowing what your family eats—both their wants and their needs—it's time to build your meal arsenal. Here's the thing: during the week you want to have recipes and meals you can rely on because you know that everyone will likely eat and enjoy the foods while being nourished and satisfied. I mentioned before that we eat pasta, and we also eat rice a lot (word to my Liberian family and Hubs's New Orleans family) and love potatoes. So I tend to build meals around making those stars or a great costar. Burgers and fries will always be a hit at my house, whether we buy or make them. Crinkle or shoestring fries are the preferred fried potatoes—steak fries did not make the cut after various tries. My mom makes us traditional Liberian food once a week—that's the perk of her living down the street—and the kids *love* it. It's always rice and some sort of stew on top. We're also huge fans of taco bowls—the kids opt out of the beans and pico but love guacamole, cheese, meat, and rice. (I make delicious cilantro lime rice.) Every season, I have about ten recipes that I make for each meal of the day and then rotate them to keep things fresh. A couple of times a month, I might try something new or introduce something new with a familiar meal, so the kids are more open to trying it.

Write your recipe down in your Notes app or on a cute recipe card you keep in a tin or binder. If dinner was a hit and it was something new, I write it down immediately.

MAGIC MEMO

Not great at cooking but looking to avoid the drive-thru? Try meal kit delivery. It's a great option because most places offer fresh (and sometimes organic) ingredients and they give you the recipe cards for every meal you order. I also like that they have options that cater to various budgets. When you learn how to make something, you can repeat what you like by buying your own ingredients next

> time and tweaking the recipe. The best part is that when you even slightly change a recipe, you make it your own. And now, you're not so bad at cooking anymore.

TRADITIONS AT THE TABLE

Eating together as a family is something that's always been important to me. We do a pretty good job with having dinner as a family at the dinner table every night. Our routine is to put everything else on the back burner while we enjoy a meal together and focus on one another. Studies have shown that families who eat together stay together. Basically, there are a slew of benefits of families eating together, whether it's breakfast, lunch, or dinner.

According to studies, children of families who eat together tend to have less anxiety; eating together encourages good eating habits (kids are more likely to eat five servings of fruits and vegetables a day); and being together at mealtime fosters a sense of belonging, safety, and security for children. Now, I understand that this is easier said than done. Between work, school, and extracurricular activities, you gotta do what you gotta do. I am radically selfish about eating with my family. I am adamant about our having at least one meal together versus treating eating together as a chore. It is quality time, time well spent, and I hope time that helps shape my kids as people because it certainly shapes me.

Honestly, I didn't even really know about the benefits of eating together when I first insisted on it. I just knew that I wanted to enjoy my family uninterrupted at least once a day. Both Chris and I come from big families that cook a lot, and whenever we have family gatherings with food it brings me so much joy. So I've tried my hardest to repeat that on a smaller scale with dinner every night.

MAGIC MEMO

At dinnertime all screens are off—TV, tablets, phones, and computers. They're not allowed at the table. Neither are any toys. The table is sacred ground for meals and conversations where we can be present. Food tastes better and conversation sounds better when it's uninterrupted.

Dinner is at 6:00 p.m. if we're on schedule, and afterward we talk with the kids about their day, play a game (we love *Heads Up!*), or have a mini after-dinner dance party. Those little moments don't seem like a big deal, but they add up. It's fun to see their sweet faces light up when Chris turns on a favorite Stevie Wonder song or a song from one of their favorite TV shows. Those moments are small yet special because they make us, us. I'm present in those moments because I know how important it is for my children to see me enjoying being with them. When I became a mom, I convinced myself that I had to be perfect. The problem is that most of us are too busy trying to show up perfect instead of being present and it's costing us purpose.

There's no way to be a perfect mom. But there are a million ways to be a good one. Being present during after-dinner dance parties is one of them.

MAGIC BUT REAL

Without question, Chris is the better cook between the two of us. I can cook; he just cooks better. Also: I'm a take-out queen. Wings, pizza, burger and fries—sign me up. I'm happy to order dinner to save time and keep my peace of mind. Our dinner doesn't matter any more when we cook a five-star meal. The dinner matters because we're together and breaking bread together. And if you ask me if I want to cook dinner or order it, I hope you're okay with hibachi takeout.

TRADITIONS OF TIME

We spend a lot of time together as a family in this current season of our lives. It's nice because the kids are small, and we are creating a lot of habits and traditions as a family that shape all of us as people. I don't take any of that for granted no matter how much work it is. One of the things we recently started doing is being deliberate about spending one-on-one time with each of the kids. I recently listened to a podcast where Jim Sheils, the author of *The Family Board Meeting*, talked about how we have only eighteen summers with our kids before they leave the house as adults. Sure, there's some give-and-take to that statement as some kids leave the house earlier or later, but it certainly put things in perspective for me. Eighteen summers is such a small piece of an entire lifetime. It made me want to make my summers, where things are usually slower-paced for the entire family, count a lot more. The standard I'd like to set is being on my phone and computer less and being present more. As I thought about it, I wondered, *Why does that have to be reserved for the summer only?* I'd like that to be the norm when I'm with my family on any day in any season. Sheils also went on to discuss how he spends one-on-one time with each of the kids every quarter. I was instantly inspired, bought his book, and prioritized one-on-ones with our kids almost immediately.

We have three kids in our family and they all enjoy different things. I wanted to make sure they had the space to do some of those things without having to compromise with the entire group. Every month, Hubs or I have a one-on-one with one of the kids. What's great about the one-on-one with your child is that all the attention is on them, and instead of rallying the troops and making sure all the kids are safe, you can be fully present to one and enjoy the person your child is. I can't encourage this enough. It has opened communication with all of our kids—even when they're very young—in a positive and lasting way.

We call it their day, and they get to pick what they want to do for a few hours and where they'd like to eat. There's something special about breaking bread with another person, so that's typically how we end the time. While breaking bread is a great time for saying one or two things to your child: "I'm proud of you" and/or "I'm sorry."

I think that a genuine moment of praise or a genuine apology from us as parents can shape our kids in ways that years of school or formal training cannot. There are few things more meaningful than a parent telling a child why they are so proud of them or apologizing for something that was hurtful to the child. Whether your kid is five or fifteen, both pride and apology matter. This one-on-one time is an opportunity for your humanity to be in the presence of your child's humanity and for you to learn about each other on a deeper level without having to share the moment with anyone else. That devoted time to get to know each other, have a shared experience, and simply talk is unmatched. The goal shouldn't be to make the moment go fast or even to overtly teach a lesson; it's a time for you to simply be and to give your child that freedom as well.

MAGIC MOMENT

"No fair! Why does she get to go with Dad?" One-on-one time will often bring out jealousy in your other kids. It certainly did with mine. Jealousy is a normal and natural emotion when you feel like you're missing out. I had to explain to my oldest, who reacted like this when she learned that her sister and dad were going out without any of us, that this was a good thing for them and that she would get the opportunity to spend time with her dad at another time. I get jealous when my kids are taking up a lot of my husband's time, which is why date night is a regular thing. Teach your children now that it's normal and okay for them not to be included in every activity, so it's not a brutal lesson they learn later in life.

You may think to yourself, *I can't believe that I haven't been spending one-on-one time with my kid. I've missed out!* The good news is you don't have to miss out anymore. If the idea of spending one-on-one time with your children resonates, make the goal moving forward to schedule it on a monthly or quarterly basis. Also, you don't have to spend a fortune to make this time with them count. If they ask to do something that isn't realistic for whatever reason, suggest something similar but within reason and your means to make it a reality for them. Sure, Disney World on Sunday isn't feasible, but maybe you can go to that really cool park downtown and get burgers at the local diner afterward. Even with modest means, you have options, and be sure to make your child feel like they do too. This is their day that they get to share with you. Doing this with them at scheduled times throughout the year not only helps them, but also might finally make your mom-guilt subside. Any way you cut it, it's a good thing that's worth making the time for.

Recently my work has been extra busy, and some days I look at my kids and feel like they're growing so fast. I'm fortunate enough to make my own schedule and be there for them most days, but on those days I'm busy with work it feels like they grow even faster. Those one-on-one days are precious to me because it's like I get to truly relish the time I have with them, even if only for a few hours. I can't be there for them all the time, but the times I am there, I'm all in.

FAMILY MEETINGS

Family meetings are important because you can discuss everything from the fun stuff—what to do on vacation—to the not-so-fun but necessary things—the budget.

That's the entire point of a family meeting—awareness of what's going on in the family, internally and externally. That means activities, budgets, well-being, and good old-fashioned conversation. Family meetings don't have to be long and strenuous, but they do have to be consistent to keep everyone aware of what's going on. Budget meetings are reserved for me and Chris, but then we like to include the kids in a general family meeting to discuss upcoming trips or events, what they'd like to do for their birthdays or the holidays, and how everyone's feeling after a big moment. (As they get older, we plan on including them in money conversations.) We typically take out a few minutes on Saturday morning to do this in the living room. This doesn't have to be overly formal, but your meeting should have some structure and be led by the person who cares about it the most. For our family, that's Chris, and he does a good job of getting straight to the point, keeping us in the loop, and asking us questions that get answers that matter.

MAGIC MEMO

This won't look the same for all families because all families are different. This isn't about fulfilling outdated gender roles because that's what you saw your parents or grandparents do or even what you saw on TV. This is about positioning yourself and your family to win. It's about putting every family member in a position where their strengths shine and to help the family collectively achieve the family mission.

Having a family mission can be one of the most groundbreaking things you do for your family. It allows you to create a clear direction, so you move collectively as a family in a way that supports your values, accomplishes goals, and makes your dreams come true. The mission of a family is to thrive collectively in agreement toward a common goal. Who doesn't want to be a part of that?

WEEKLY SCREEN FAST

From 6:00 p.m. on Friday to 6:00 p.m. on Saturday, we turn off and put away all screens at our house. TVs, tablets, phones, computers—they're all off-limits. You pretty much have no choice but to talk and play with one another, which has certainly brought us closer together as a family. Because the kids are so young, I'm excited about normalizing for them that being away from devices for a day to be present can still be a time to enjoy yourself.

The average adult spends three hours and forty-three minutes on their phone every day. Without a doubt, I spend way more time on my phone than that since I create online content for a living. But let's just say I was average—three hours and forty-three minutes is long enough for you to have watched *Avengers: Endgame* and taken a forty-minute nap. That's a lot of time. Also, I have a fear of my kids remembering me as the mom who paid more attention to her phone than them. I really don't want that.

Listen, I have no problem telling my kids that "Mommy has to get some work done" and doing just that. But if I know how to tell them that I need to get work done, when do I tell work that I need to go be with my family? They need to see me pick them over work more often than sporadically. My family needs to know that work is important but that they are a priority because of the intentional boundaries I've put in place. A line has to be drawn. The screen fast has become a version of that line.

"So, what do you do during a screen fast?" is often the question I get. Absolutely any and everything else that doesn't require a screen. We do crafts, paint, read, write, organize, purge, and—wait for it—just sit down and talk. Like the kind of talking where you're actually engaged and look in each other's eyes because you're really interested in what the person is saying. It's a skill I don't want to lose and a skill I want my kids to have. Don't just be interesting, be interested.

MAGIC BUT REAL

While this screen fast is great for a multitude of reasons, I've also found myself being preoccupied with chores or tasks during this time. The whole point of the screen fast is to pay more attention to your family. Spending me time and taking care of household chores can certainly be done during this time, but they shouldn't be prioritized over quality time with the kids. If I'm organizing the pantry because the kids are playing in the playroom and they ask me to play, I'm playing. The pantry will always be there. My two-year-old pretending to be Spider-Man while I'm the villain—that will happen only for a short while. This is easier said than done, I'll admit, but it's worth it.

Once it's 6:00 p.m. on Saturday, we can bring on the screens. And, typically, we break our fast with a family movie night.

MOVIE NIGHT

Saturday night is movie night at our house. It's a weekly family tradition we all really lean into. Like I explained earlier, growing up I had movie night on Friday night with my parents and sister. I couldn't even tell you what movies we watched, I just remember my dad popping microwavable popcorn (I know it's not the best for you, but what salty deliciousness) and eating strawberry shortcake biscuits. It was a time of togetherness that made me feel safe, that made me feel like I belonged, and I cherished it so much. It was a moment just for us.

As I write these words, I'm realizing that my present-day movie night with my own family is in a way me re-creating that time from my childhood. A moment of togetherness that hopefully will live rent-free in my kids' heads and hearts. We are that ridiculous family who has almost every streaming service, so we have our own Blockbuster right at our fingertips. We let the kids pick whatever movie they want to watch. We do the picking in the morning or afternoon just in case there is much deliberation.

Because it's movie night and we have a big homemade breakfast on Saturday morning, we typically do takeout for dinner on movie night. It's usually pepperoni pizza, which is a big hit with all three of my kids in this current season. We do dinner around 6:00 p.m., bathe everyone, and then they get out their sleeping bags and pillows for the movie. We have a sectional that has a pullout sleeper, and the kids love to lie on it with their sleeping bags. Last but not least, snacks.

One thing my kids are very excited about on movie night is the snacks. It's all my fault. One time I made a movie night snack board, and that has been the expectation ever since. We're a huge popcorn family, but one night I thought it'd be cool to do two different types of popcorn with some fruit (grapes and strawberries), M&M's, and Oreos on one of our wooden cutting boards. It really raised the stakes.

Here's the thing—I love creating a charcuterie board. In fact, I'll charcuterie anything. Just last weekend, I charcuteried (yes, I know—that's not an actual word) pound cake and organized cut fruit into ROYGBIV and added a little bowl with whipped cream.

Beautifully presented snacks matter to us. So that's what we do for movie night.

If your family is dedicated to the variety of KitKat bars, try a new flavor every week. Maybe chips and dip are what you are into, so have fun with it. But whatever you enjoy, find a way to magnify it during your family moments. It will take your family moment or tradition to the next level.

PLAYING OUTSIDE

Making sure the entire family spends time together outside at least once a week really makes a huge difference. First of all, it's a huge mood booster. When the sun hits your face, no matter what season it is, it literally makes you feel better. (Yeah, even on an overcast day.) **Sunlight releases serotonin (the happiness hormone)** in your brain, boosts your bone health, and actually might help treat several skin conditions. Without sun exposure, your serotonin levels dip, which can be associated with a higher risk of major depression and generally feeling down in the dumps.

Being outside with your family makes you happy with the people you love the most. It's the draw 4 card, the big joker, the checkmate of life. And what I love most about this activity is that it doesn't have to be reserved for a specific day. You can do this on the weekend or on a weekday after everyone gets home from school and work. Don't have a front yard or backyard? No worries. Find a local park or field nearby where you can play soccer or a serious round of tag. Sometimes you don't even need a "game" per se. Nothing riles up my kids more than me or Chris saying, "I'm going to get you!"

I've been really committed to getting in my ten thousand steps (adulthood, is that you?), and we recently discovered a nearby park that has a track. Hubs and I take turns watching the kids at the playground while the other walks a couple of miles. It feels great.

Let me also add that this is not reserved for summer either. Sure, spring and summer weather is typically ideal for outdoor activities, but you can play outside in the fall and winter too. Fall has some beautiful cool days that feel so good. And when it's winter, put those coats and gloves on and enjoy. If you live in a location where it snows, that's even more incentive. Play outside with your kids. Release yourself from the monotony of adulthood for twenty to thirty minutes. Plus, I love creating a memory where my kids get to say, "I played outside with my mom today."

Aside from this being great physical activity for you and everyone in your family, it's a good way to guarantee everyone actually falls asleep when their head hits the pillow at night. It's a win-win.

At the end of the day, it's not about being a perfect mom with a perfect family. But wow, we sure have had a lot of MAGIC moments together as a family. Not because they were expensive or fancy or even something that other people would enjoy. Mostly it's because we've created moments that gave us space to be present, together, and authentically ourselves. There are no two families that are exactly alike, but we can all benefit from living what we love, spending time and making MAGIC, together.

CHAPTER FIVE

Tasks Can Be
MAGIC Too

*Make a list and check it twice to make sure
you've only listed what matters.*

Growing up, I remember Mom always had a "Things to Do" list. She called it her "brains," and I truly can't recall her starting her day without it. She'd get her coffee, grab her datebook (I love that she called it that) or even a scrap piece of paper if her datebook wasn't around, and write down her tasks for the day.

No matter what day it was—during the week or on the weekend—she jotted down a handful of things to get done within the day. She never made a move before making this list. To this day, as a grandmother, she still operates this way and gets the most done without breaking a sweat. Some people look up to fictional superheroes. I look up to my mom—the woman, the legend, who always writes things down so she never forgets or stresses out trying to remember what tasks she needs to complete.

Call the dentist
Pick up butter
Drop off dry cleaning

The woman is a to-do list wiz. She taught me the importance of writing a "Things to Do" list, and after watching it bring her so much success, I swear by having my own everyday "brains."

I write everything down. Because if I don't, I will forget.

Mom's generation had way fewer distractions to deal with than we currently have, and she still wrote everything down to ensure she got things done.

Nowadays our attention is pulled in too many directions to try to remember what we have to do. Between email, social media notifications, remembering the Netflix password, email, the kids' schedules, email, Chris's schedule, email, my own schedule, content deadlines, email, meetings, the 24/7 news cycle, and you can't forget email—there's just way too much going on to not write it down.

Here's the other thing: We're busier than ever. There is so much to get done, for home, for the kids, for our village, for work, and oh yeah, we have to make time for self-care as well. There's your dentist appointment, the kids' recital at school, your best friend's birthday, that big meeting for work, and trying to catch up on the new season of your favorite Netflix show all in the same week. And guess what? Each of those tasks can be MAGIC. Your life tasks can be MAGIC. Yep, even going to the dentist. But that list of things to do doesn't even count the tasks you tackle to function day to day or the extra things that will inevitably come up. (Things that come up aren't necessarily a bad thing, just a real-life, that's-how-life-works thing.) Being present in those moments to execute, appreciate, or resolve each of those tasks already requires quite a bit of mental bandwidth, so you want to set yourself up for success as much as you can.

Having full days or even full weeks with tons of things to tackle is sometimes inevitable. Busy seasons that require hard work and valiant effort will come and go. Feeling overburdened seems like it has to be a part of the equation, but it really doesn't. As someone who has ugly cried because she had to load the dishwasher after a really long day, I absolutely get it. Sometimes you're going to have those days and it's part of being human.

Let me say this: you're doing a good job. You have a lot on your plate and I want you to give yourself both grace and credit. Sometimes you're going to have those days and it's part of being human. But if you find yourself constantly feeling on the edge, day after day, it's worth stepping back and asking, "What actually matters? What's not working? What do I need to do to make what matters work?"

The season of going from one to two kids whooped my ass. I

won't even lie to you. It was incredibly overwhelming because my business started to grow rapidly while my family did at the same time, and I just felt like I was drowning. I felt like I was always missing the mark with someone in my family—the new baby, my preschooler, or my husband—and I was constantly blowing deadlines without communicating that I needed more time. It was embarrassing because I saw how other women—people I knew and others I saw on social media—had families and seemed to function just fine. And in the first six months after having my second baby, I was a mess. I remember looking out the window and thinking, *How have women been doing this forever?!*

Turns out that you can have a full plate and get what matters done without sacrificing your everyday MAGIC (and sanity)—by writing things down, batching, asking for help, hiring help, or simply saying no. Your daily tasks don't have to be the enemy. With the right approach for you, not only can you get what matters done, your tasks can be MAGIC too.

MAGIC MEMO

What is a task? A task is a piece of work to be done or undertaken. This can reference anything from making dinner to closing a deal. But for further clarity, here's what tasks mean throughout this chapter. I believe there are micro tasks, routine tasks, and macro tasks.

Micro task: a task that takes you less than five minutes to complete and/or does not require your undivided attention

Routine task: a task that you do on a daily, weekly, or frequent basis

Macro task: a task that takes five minutes or longer and/or requires your undivided attention

CAPTURE NOW; REFERENCE LATER

The number one reason why we don't get things done is because there are way too many distractions competing for our attention. Basically, there are too many open tabs in your head and you can barely focus on one tab because you're too busy thinking about several other open ones.

Anytime we promise ourselves we'll remember things, we don't. At least, I don't. We simply do not have the capacity. It's not because we're dumb, lazy, or incompetent. It's because we have too much to remember while resisting so many distractions.

You don't get a medal for perfectly remembering things, you get credit only for what you get done. What I've learned is that you don't have to remember it; instead, you can reference it. But you can reference only what you capture. This is why I'm a firm believer in "capture now; reference later." I'm here to turn you into a believer too.

To successfully capture, you'll have to be intentional and present. Capturing is briefly pausing and simply taking the laundry list of tasks in your head and writing it down. It doesn't need to be written down perfectly. It doesn't even have to be pretty. It just needs to be done so you can reference it later when you have time to think or it's time to get the work done. Anytime you capture a task that needs to be done, you close a tab in your head. The reason you have to start with closing all the open tabs in your head is because it positions you to think freely and purely. That's when your best ideas, purposeful clarity, excellent work, and even your short- and long-term memories get to shine. When you have the freedom to tackle tasks by being present, you find the joy in doing the work. Because tasks—whether they're micro, routine, or macro—require ample mental space to execute, the more tabs you close in your head, the more mental space you have available to execute at a high level. When you have more mental space, you can be more present. When you're more present, you're more mindful about what you're doing. When you're more mindful, you're more likely to execute with excellence—at anything. Packing for a trip, writing an email, serious conversation, working out, you name it.

Tasks matter, but only when you remember what they are and execute them. Don't hold yourself hostage trying to remember all the things that can simply be written down to look over later. If what you have to get done is actually meaningful and important to you—no matter how big or small it is—then write it down. (Or type it into your phone.) It's better to write than to be wrong. The faintest ink is better than the best memory.

MAGIC BUT REAL

Yes, writing things down is good, but don't go overboard. Not every task needs to be written down. Tasks like taking out the trash, brushing your teeth, and taking a shower may not need to go on your list since they're routine.

Whenever you close the tabs in your head, you open yourself to being excellent at your tasks at hand. Freeing up space in your head is meaningful because you're no longer being held hostage by future tasks to complete.

For so long, we've been taught to multitask to get more done, faster. But what if you got less done, better? You'd feel better while doing better. That's the power of capturing so you can reference later.

Capturing happens in real time. Referencing happens at a designated time. For instance, the ideas in this book have come to me at random times in my life—the shower, right before bed, first thing in the morning, and even during a road trip. Realistically, I couldn't write this book at all of those times. But I wrote the ideas down when I had them. Capturing is timely, but referencing is tedious and requires more uninterrupted time so you can flesh out an idea or execute the task.

To be clear, I don't capture everything. Just the ideas that matter for myself, my family, home, life, or work. The ideas that are meaningful to me or someone who matters to me, or that obviously help me accomplish a specific goal, make me want to take action. Basically, if the idea isn't MAGIC, I don't really bother myself with it. Just because I can, doesn't mean I should.

MAGIC MEMO

When an idea comes to you, grab your phone or notebook (or a sticky note) and jot it down. Try to keep it stored in your head for as short a time as possible. The sooner you release the idea by capturing it, the sooner you can get back to having ample mental space. Another reason why you want to capture an idea as soon as possible is so that your memory doesn't dilute the purity of it.

Suppose I come up with an idea for my daughter's birthday party. I'm probably excited about it and the fresh idea is vivid and potent in my head. The longer I hold it in my head and think about it—versus capturing the idea—the greater the chances are that it will be muted by whatever distractions are near. Then the energy I take to fight off a distraction and remember the clarity of my idea of a birthday party theme is strained. So by the time I capture it six hours later, I'm asking myself the proverbial question, "What was the idea I had?" And now, my eight-year-old might have a mediocre birthday theme all because I didn't capture the idea ASAP.

The sooner you can capture a fresh idea that you know you'll want to revisit later because you're preoccupied in the moment, the better.

So now that you have all of these ideas captured, when do you reference them? You reference them at one of two times: during "thinking time" or "time of task." We will discuss thinking time later—it's the time in the morning or whatever productive part of your day that you've scheduled uninterrupted time to think. What are you thinking about? Everything you've written down in the last twenty-four hours or even the last week. When you're referencing these things, you likely have fresh eyes thanks to a renewed mind. Now, you have the capacity to be honest with yourself about whether you really want to act on an idea. This is when you decide if an idea is worth taking out of your MAGIC hat because it honors, applies to, or teaches you. Or you may decide you should put it back because it doesn't do any of those things for you. That's what makes thinking time so special. Time to think gives you space to be honest.

The great thing about closing the tabs in your head and capturing things is that it is so simple. It simply requires you to take whatever is in your head and write it down (physically or digitally) in a place you can easily reference later. It should be the same place you reference things regularly, so it isn't overlooked.

If you regularly jot down things in your Notes app, keep your captures there. Don't feel the need to write them in a fancy new app because lots of your friends suggested it. If there's a notebook you always have around, write in that. The key is to write your notes somewhere you will very likely revisit.

This isn't where I tell you that analog or digital is better. But I will encourage you to do what comes naturally to you so you're more likely to do it. So, if writing your things-to-do list in Google Drive is your natural capture rhythm, run with it. You can even jot down your idea, task, or whatever else you need to remember in your phone and physically write it down later. I'm a mix of both; I like both digital and analog. Lately, I've been leaning more toward digital because it allows me to both easily edit and access my ideas at any given time. The flexibility of digital works best for me now.

You might be the person who always has a little notebook with them and writing it physically works best. Let's be honest—buying pretty notebooks and planners is fun. It's sort of like a materialistic incentive to write things down. Again, aesthetics definitely contribute to your everyday MAGIC, so have fun with them. You like floral pens? Buy them. You like gold spiral-bound planners with tabs? Get them. But let's actually put them to good use so we don't become victims of consumerism.

Just commit to stop trying to remember everything. It serves no one, especially when you forget a million-dollar idea, the birthday of someone you love, or that appointment you had booked for months.

SLAYING YOUR DAY

A few years ago, my pastor discussed the story of David. Since I was a child, I have always been fascinated by the story of David slaying Goliath. It's never not interesting to me, and I learn a new lesson from the story every time I hear it. In this instance, Pastor discussed how we should take on our own Goliaths with faith and confidence like David. He said, "David your Goliath," and I've made it one of my personal mantras since.

In the day-to-day, "David your Goliath" means "Do the hardest thing first." Tackle the giant task first. The task that would make you cuss in front of your momma—knock it out before lunchtime. That makes the rest of your day much easier. Now, many people have argued that David was able to defeat Goliath because of his training, but in my opinion, he was able to defeat the giant because of his mindset.

David made up his mind that he was going to slay Goliath before he slung one stone. That's the same mentality that I like to walk into every day with. Whether it's meal planning, negotiating a deal with a brand partner, or having a hard conversation with a loved one—I like to start with what's hard or difficult, so I can breeze through the rest of my day.

That being said, schedule only one Goliath a day. There will be those anomalies of days where there will be more than one that you can't avoid, but if it works out, tackle only one Goliath and tackle it first.

When David knew he had to slay the giant, he went and gathered five stones to get the job done. That's the same way you have to slay your day.

We've discussed that you should do the hardest task of your day first, but let's discuss how many tasks you should be doing. Have you ever looked at your things-to-do list at the end of the day and you've done only two of those things? Or even worse, you had twelve things on your list, but you only got a little bit of each thing done? Yeah, it doesn't feel great. Here are the brutal facts:

You're putting way too many things on your things-to-do list. Way too many things.

Putting five tasks on your things-to-do list is more than enough. Yes, you read that right. *Five.*

If David needed only five stones to defeat Goliath, you need only five tasks on your to-do list to make it count.

Your day doesn't have to be jam-packed for it to matter. You don't get credit for how many things are on your things-to-do list. You get credit for what gets done. It's time to start aiming for putting only things on your list that you'll complete at 100 percent.

It's all about slaying your day. Not suffocating it. When you wrap up your day, you should be pleased with the tasks you completed. That shouldn't be all the things. Just the things that matter. You're only one person. You don't need to be stretched thin to be valued.

Also, there's nothing more beautiful than a complete things-to-do list with all your tasks of the day crossed off and completed. By putting only five things on your list, you increase your chances of doing that daily.

DELEGATE WHAT YOU HATE

One day on Instagram Stories, I went on a tangent about how effective my laundry routine was. How I sort, how I wash almost everything on the cold cycle, how I fold to increase the likelihood of not pulling clean clothes out of the hamper for the next week. The advice was good.

But the truth was I hate doing laundry. Even though I'm good at it—I hate it.

My big-sister-in-my-head, Myleik, messaged me something that

I'll never forget. She simply asked, "Why don't you just get your laundry done? It'll save you so much time and it's criminally cheap. Plus, with three small children it'll give you a break."

Almost immediately I asked her who she used and I booked the service that same day. She was right. I could absolutely use the break and it was criminally cheap. Honestly, for as much as I hate doing laundry, I was expecting the service to be a couple hundred dollars a week. (Which I would've gladly paid.) Turns out, for my family of five, it costs me $40 a week for about four loads of laundry. Even in our hectic weeks when we have bigger loads, it still doesn't come up to more than $50.

Listen, I would eat PB&J for dinner every night of the week to save that $200 to avoid doing laundry.

MAGIC MEMO

Delegate what you hate.

And for the last couple of years, with the exception of linens or towels whenever we have a spill or an accident, I haven't done laundry. It's bought me so much more time and I get to spend that time with my family or simply just relax. At the risk of sounding extra, it's added some years to my life. I don't stress about having to get laundry done because on Wednesday they pick it up and they drop it off every Thursday. Yes—they literally drop it off the next day.

Here's what really freed me to act on Myleik's suggestion of getting laundry service—I realized that yes, laundry needs to be done every week or so. It just doesn't have to be done *by me.*

This idea of always doing everything traps a lot of us and we end up missing out on the MAGIC in our lives. What's the point of creating a life of MAGIC if we're only going to be consumed by micromanaging ourselves out of living?!

We do it to ourselves all the time and then wonder why we're exhausted. It's because we're trying to do it all and failing every time we do. Once you understand that "doing it all" is not a requirement to having a full life, you are free. If you have a full plate, portion out the work by deciding what must get done and then delegate to those who are willing to help you or hired to help.

Before you delegate, you have to decide what is even worth doing. The last thing you want to do is ask or hire help for something that doesn't even matter to you, your family, or your life. Getting clarity on what matters is always worth a pause and asking yourself the following questions:

Is this a priority?

If it's not, and you hate doing it, guess what? You can and should say no to it. Laundry is a priority because we need to wear clean clothes every day. There's no flexibility around that. So if your task is a priority, then ask yourself the next question.

How much time does it require?

If it takes more than an hour to complete *and* you hate it, it's a time suck. Spending time doing things we don't enjoy isn't proof that we're good or responsible. Laundry usually takes anywhere from three to four hours total a week if you count sorting, washing, folding, and putting away. A total time suck.

How often does it need to be done?

Because there are five of us at my house, if laundry piles up for more than a week, it becomes a real chore. Weekly is the schedule preference for laundry being done at our house. Decide what your preference is and then maintain it.

Do you have anyone in your life right now who has time to help you with this?

If a task takes two hours, do you know anyone who can help you or simply complete the task for you? Laundry is a daunting task for most and takes a lot of time. I don't have anyone in my life who can or would want to help with this, so I chose to hire it out. If you have older kids who can handle their own laundry, delegate it to them. Dividing and delegating tasks to your family helps you to manage how much time a task takes since it's being done by more than one person.

Do you have the means to hire help for the task without it affecting your daily standard of living?

If you have no one to help you, the best thing to do is look at options to hire help. I looked up local laundry services but ended up using my friend's referral of her laundry lady.

If you're in the position to hire help, do it. This does not make you bougie or elitist. Especially because we don't treat those who help us (whether they're asked or hired) like we're better than them.

Because we're not.

There is no shame in hiring help, especially when you can afford it. When you do, you're usually helping a small business and putting food on someone's table. That is a good thing.

My first laundry lady was the best. The laundry service was her small business and she had three kids like I did. When she picked up and dropped off, we'd always briefly catch up like old friends. After about five months or so, she moved because her husband's job was transferred to another state. I was heartbroken—but focused. Two weeks before her service ended, I did some research and found another local laundry service thanks to a referral from my sister. The pricing was almost identical and incredibly reasonable.

Every week, I pay between $35 and $50 to have my laundry done for my family of five. They pick up Wednesday and drop off the next day for no extra charge. Because my laundry is returned folded and sorted, putting it away is simple and fast.

And instead of trying to seem like the perfect wife and mother who does laundry in a timely manner even though she hates it, I delegate it for the cost of takeout. Not only that, now I can spend more time doing things I enjoy with my family. It doesn't get more MAGIC than that.

I am very grateful that I have options and I understand that's not everyone's reality. Before I delegated my laundry, I batched it, like I do so many of the tasks at home (and in life!).

BATCH, PLEASE

Let's face it, even if you do delegate what you hate, there are still a bunch of everyday tasks that have to get done in real time that you will likely not be able to hire out. Sure, the kids can help, and even your spouse, but let's face it: if you want it done "your way" and done fast, you'll have to do it. I don't like it when mundane tasks take me a long time to do. I'd rather play in traffic barefoot and blindfolded. This is why I'm so dedicated to batch-processing tasks, because it creates the MAGIC of doing things faster and more efficiently.

You don't have to be "good" at household tasks, just efficient. Batching is when you do similar tasks with similar tools to get more done faster. It is the antithesis of multitasking and you will be so happy when you apply it to household tasks. There are certain tasks I do every day or every week that proceed more efficiently when I batch—such as unloading the dishwasher, clearing the dinner table, putting together meals, and putting away the groceries.

Batching Unloading the Dishwasher

Growing up with my West African mother, the dishwasher was simply the drying rack. From the age of seven I learned how to wash the dishes by hand and believed that nothing but clean dishes should be in the dishwasher. Even to this day, if I have dirty dishes in my dishwasher, my mom will wash what she used, dry it, and put it away. She just refuses to put a dirty dish in the dishwasher. It makes me laugh to my core. I am not that way anymore. The dishwasher is an active participant in my home and I gladly welcome it. I run the dishwasher every night after dinner. Even with a dishwasher doing all the heavy lifting, you still have to empty and load the dishwasher. There's not one thing exciting about emptying the dishwasher or loading it, so you just have to get it done. The faster I can get it done, the better for me. What I've realized is that unloading the dishwasher can become busywork if I don't batch it.

To batch the unloading of the dishwasher, I take all of the clean dishes out of the dishwasher and put them on the counter and organize them by where they're going. So all of our mason jars go in one area on the counter, all the kids cups and plates in another, and then all the coffee mugs, and so on. I organize all the clean dishes on the counter first before putting any of them away. That's the thing about batching, you complete one step all at the same time before moving on to the next one. Once everything is out of the dishwasher and on the counter, I then put all the clean dishes in the cabinets or drawers where they belong. However, because I've grouped like with like on the counter, the putting-away step of the process now moves along noticeably faster versus putting some forks up, then mugs, then a bowl, then a mug again. Once all the mugs are put away, that's it. I don't have to go to that same cabinet over and over again. When all the silverware is put away, it's done.

Batching Clearing the Table

Eating dinner together is one of those everyday MAGIC moments that really make our family feel like our true selves. We all enjoy it, but when we're done with it, I go into Shut It Down mode. Clearing the table can become another busywork task where I'm going to the fridge, to the sink, to the fridge, to the trash can, to the sink again; and I simply feel scattered by the end of it. Batch-clearing of the table allows me to group like tasks and get more done, more efficiently. That's the name of the game here.

When I clear the dinner table, I clear all the fridge and cabinet items first. Things like butter, dressing, salt, and pepper get put away first. For my next mini-batch, I take any remaining leftover food from the meal and package it up. This mini-batch works great because when I ask the kids to help me clear the table, I can have them work on another mini-batch—the dirty dishes. In this mini-batch, you do just what you'd expect: clear all the dishes from the table, discard any remaining food on the plates into the trash, and then put the dirty dishes in the sink. The last mini-batch is cleaning the table and the floor—that includes wiping down the table, then sweeping the floor. Once that's done, I can get into batching the dishes and loading them into the dishwasher.

MAGIC BUT REAL

I will fight anyone who puts leftovers in a cooking pot in my fridge. It doesn't make any sense, takes up too much space in the refrigerator, and is so annoying when you need a pot but it's holding leftovers. Also, leftovers just belong in containers. So, there's that.

Batching Putting Together Meals

Right now, two out of our three kids go to school and I make their lunch most days. Making their lunch is something I like to do and it's a way for me to make heart-shaped sandwiches and slip in sweet notes that say "I love you." (Yes, I'm that mom.) Deciding ahead of time what we're going to eat the next day helps out a lot. Decision fatigue is a real thing. And I'm a firm believer that making **small-ass decisions (SADs)** in real time kills our productivity. Any SADs that must be made every day—what to eat, what to wear, et cetera—should be made ahead of time to spare you decision fatigue.

One thing that we all have to do, no matter how differently we do it, is eat breakfast, lunch, and dinner. I don't like to think too much about what we're going to eat for any meal, so I've come up with a little acronym—EATS—to help me rotate different options.

E is for entrée

The entrée is the main character of the EATS plate. Typically, it's a protein source, and because our family eats meat it's normally chicken, turkey, or fish. But no matter what your family's diet is, the entrée serves as the anchor of the meal. You pick the entrée and then build the rest of the meal around it. If your family is pescatarian, entrées could include baked salmon or shrimp tacos. If you're vegan, it could be spiraled zucchini or black bean burgers. The goal here is to figure out what your family's go-to entrées are for the season and keep them in rotation.

A is for appetizer

Next, I add an appetizer or side to a meal. For a school lunch, that's typically a snack. They have a snack time before lunch, so I often send something with healthy fats (yogurt or string cheese) or something nutritious (applesauce or cucumber slices with dressing). I try to send a snack that'll actually hold them over until it's time for lunch. For breakfast or dinner, I'll add a carb like pasta, potatoes, rice, or bread.

An appetizer is simply something that complements or balances out the entrée. If the entrée is a taco or a quesadilla, the appetizer could be rice and beans. If the entrée is a turkey and cheese sandwich, the appetizer could be potato chips. The beauty of the appetizer is that there is no wrong choice. It really works when it's something that complements the entrée. You're just trying to give the entrée a solid plus-one.

T is for treat

No matter your stance as a parent, you understand that kids enjoy treats. It's just the thing. I'm proud to say that my kids enjoy fruits and eat their dinner, but they still love a sweet treat. I don't blame them. Sweet treats are delightful. Treats don't always have to be processed sugar. A treat can be fruit like strawberries with whipped cream, but for the most part kids want fruit snacks, Oreos, graham crackers, or the "C" word—candy. I'm all for a treat, but in moderation. (And I know, all of our definitions of "moderation" are likely different.) I like to incorporate a treat with at least one meal every day. Sometimes it's sprinkles in the pancakes we're having for breakfast or strawberries after dinner. It's all about balance. I'll do any little thing that can make a treat somewhat nutritionally better—like buying or making the organic version—without sacrificing the "treatness" of it.

S is for sustenance

At the end of the day, we have to keep it cute and healthy when it comes to meals. And even when we don't feel like it, we need fruits and vegetables, which is what I refer to as sustenance. We need something that's alive that will nourish our bodies. My kids love fresh fruit, but I try my best to get at least one to two servings of vegetables in their meals every day. I buy fruits and vegetables that are in season and that the kids actually eat. We usually don't have too much pushback on broccoli and green beans, but spinach and brussels sprouts are a big "no" for them right now. Corn, beans, and carrots have their shining moments sometimes, so I incorporate them whenever it makes sense to do so. I'm not above sneaking some shredded spinach into a cheese quesadilla if I have to!

If you made an EATS hit list for your family, what would be on it?

What are the entrées your family gravitates toward for meals?

How about appetizers?

How about treats?

What about sustenance?

Here's what I love about the EATS method: It works during the holidays and during the summer when the kids are off from school. It allows me to give everyone a little bit of balance for each meal. It just works.

The whole point of batching school lunches is to pack all of the same kind of thing at once. Even if the kids are each taking a different entrée (due to allergies or preferences), you can still make all the entrées at once, then the appetizers, and so forth. It's not less work, but because you've batched them, your effort gets you results with order and efficiency.

MAGIC MOMENT

"Mom, can I help?" Just like with a cooking chore, whenever one of the kids asks to help me do something I usually batch, I let them. This of course means I have to slow down to teach them how to properly do something. Sometimes that means I have to take my time to explain something when the inevitable "why?" is asked and then give them a physical example of how to do a task. While I'm all about personal productivity, I value present moments with my kids more. Teaching kids how to do chores or household tasks makes them feel like part of the team (which they are!) and shows them that they are capable. Maizah knows how to clear the table and Caliana loves helping me load plastic and kid-friendly dishes in the dishwasher. They both love helping me pack lunches as well. Things move noticeably slower when they help because of giggles and the time it takes to teach them how to do things properly, but that's more than okay. My oldest helps more consistently as she gets older, and my job is to be patient with her as she learns. If for whatever reason we're in a time crunch and I need to get something done fast, I explain and tell her we'll do it together the next day—then I'm sure to keep my promise. But if there's no need to rush, slowing down so the family can help is always a good thing because it's meaningful.

Batching Putting Away the Groceries

I am definitely in a life season where I order my groceries. Things for work are busy, I have three small children, and, honestly, finding the energy to go to the grocery store myself is often a lost cause. If you have the luxury of paying for the convenience of ordering groceries and having them delivered, I encourage you to do so. It's worth it. What's great is that many grocery stores offer free delivery. My best friend, Erica, swears by delivery on a weekly basis.

Now, when the groceries get to my house my counters are cleared so I can batch in putting them away. Again, I don't like things to feel painstakingly slow or tedious, so this system is great for my personality.

On a cleared counter, I take every grocery item out of all the bags. I organize the groceries on the counter into three sections—to go in the fridge, to stay on the counter, and to go in the pantry. This may look different for you depending on how you store your food. Organize accordingly. Once everything is out, I immediately put any frozen items in the freezer. Next the fridge. This is also when I take old leftovers and any expired food out of our refrigerator. Putting groceries away is a golden opportunity for a mini fridge purge.

Once I'm done with the fridge groceries, I put away items that go on the counter or in the cabinets. Last, I put away all the pantry items. (I've given my oldest the task of delivering any personal or household items that need to go to other rooms; this makes her feel a part of the process.)

When you do something every day or every week, even if you're disciplined, be intentional about finding the most efficient way to do it to use your time wisely, which may be batching the process.

ASK FOR HELP

There is nothing wrong with asking for help. In fact, I encourage you to ask for help consistently. I'm speaking of asking for help from anyone inside of your home and even close friends or family who don't live with you. While it's easy to assume that the people who know you best—your spouse, your roommate, your kids (older than five), your bestie—should know when you need help, we all know what assuming does. Ask for help when you need it instead of harboring resentment toward those who didn't help you when you never asked.

You can get money back, but you can never get time back. This is why it's vital to respect anyone's time. (Think about how much you hate having your time wasted.) When you ask for help, be clear on exactly what you need help with and overestimate how much time it'll take. For instance, if you need help clearing out your garage and think it'll take three hours, ask for five hours of their time instead.

Asking for help from someone outside your home is usually best for a one-time or once-in-a-while task. Occasional tasks like clearing out your garage, moving, putting together furniture, or watching over your kids or pets are examples of when to ask for outside help if it's available to you. That way you won't put a strain on your relationships.

If it's a task that needs to be done weekly or even monthly, I highly recommend batching it, delegating it as a chore to your family, or, if you can, hiring it out.

If you currently have a modest budget, asking for help is great. And it's important to recognize that in certain seasons you're going to need to ask for help more than usual. When you do, be respectful and honest with whoever has decided to help you and allow them to do just that—help.

Both my husband and I come from large families and we have the most incredible friend village. We're so grateful for them all, but we go out of our way to not take advantage of their love for us.

Yes, there will be some seasons where you may have to lean on your friend village more than usual, but for the most part, ask only if you must.

Here's my other tip: When you ask for help, pay with a meal. Whether you cook it for them, take them out to eat, or even order takeout, food is always welcomed and appreciated.

Last, go out of your way to say "Thank you." I know this goes without saying, but I'd rather risk sounding redundant than have you sound ungrateful. I don't care if it's your mom, your first cousin, or your best friend from kindergarten. Make sure you express your thanks for their help. Sending a thank-you card a few days afterward is also a nice gesture.

The point of creating routines and processes isn't solely to make your day-to-day easier, it's also so your day-to-day efforts are worth it. Being able to look at your home at the end of the day and see that it's clear and in order—ready to receive you and your family the next day—is a result worth working toward. Clear space = clear mind, and if you ask me, a clear heart. Having a clear heart toward your tasks and daily work means you have no grievances and nothing but gratefulness, space, and the opportunity to enjoy it.

The long and the short of it is that you can make your tasks MAGIC by writing them down, slaying your day with five things, delegating what you hate, batching routine tasks, and asking for help consistently.

CHAPTER SIX

Time Is MAGIC

Make time for what matters.

Most of us feel like there's never enough time. The days are full for a variety of reasons. Even on weekends—in some cases especially—there is so much to do thanks to extracurricular activities and other calendar-filling events and tasks. Sure, there's lots to do, but when you start believing that time is a gift, that time is MAGIC, you'll start to use time in a much more productive way.

Maybe you're always hurrying and late, or even if you are an on-time person, you feel like you don't have enough time to finish what you start and you're always having to start and stop. Have you ever just stared off, thinking about how much time you need to tackle everything on your list for the week? Or even the day? It can make you tired before you even begin. But what if you changed your mind about time and started using it a little differently?

What I'm about to tell you won't change time. While I wish I was that brilliant, sixty seconds will always make a minute, sixty minutes will always make an hour, and twenty-four hours will always equal a day. Time is time and it cannot be changed. But you can change your mind about time. There are so many sayings and phrases that make it seem like time is our enemy when it is really one of our greatest assets in our everyday lives.

Killing time.
Time is flying.
Wasting time.
As time goes by.
Make more time.
Never enough time.

Whenever we mention time, it's always getting away from us, or we're being told we're misusing it or need much more of it. In the phrases just mentioned, take out the word "time" and replace it with your name. Imagine if that's how people talked about you every day. You wouldn't want to be more for them, would you? Do you think that's why we have so many negative thoughts surrounding time? Time is such a gift that many of us feel entitled to. How you think about time reflects how you use it. Be encouraged and start genuinely being grateful for the time you have. It's never too late to renew your mind.

Waking up every morning is a blessing. Spending time with loved ones is such a treat, even on hard days. Doing work throughout your day (even if it's not your dream job) for pay is a privilege that many people do not have. Let's stop looking at time like it's always running out and thinking that we "have" to do this, that, and the other. You get to live your life every day. If it's not the life you want, you can do the necessary work to make every day MAGIC and design the life you want. In this chapter, we'll discuss how you can use your time to create routines, schedules, and moments that infuse MAGIC throughout your everyday.

Let's be clear, your time shouldn't be spent solely working every waking minute to get things done and plan for the next day. Time is an opportunity for you to be, to live, and to enjoy the life you've created and everything you've chosen to be in it. While it's tempting to use your time solely to do things for others, it's important to start the day spending time with yourself.

As someone who was born at 10:09 in the evening, by nature I am a night owl. I'll admit, I've run myself a bath at 11:30 p.m. and not even thought twice about it. I'll stay in that bath for thirty to forty minutes without hesitation and then attempt to wake at my usual early morning time. Here's what you should know: when I stay up late and ignore the boundaries I adamantly set for myself, everyone in my house (especially me!) pays for it. I'm not nice when I'm tired;

I'm noticeably less focused so I'm less efficient, and I drag throughout the day.

I'm a night owl by nature but a morning person by choice. Why? Because getting an early start to spend time with myself matters.

Think about your everyday life—when do you get to spend time with yourself uninterrupted without having to tackle tasks for life and work? There aren't too many of those moments, are there? When you get to be by yourself for a time, you have the opportunity to be yourself. This creates space to be much kinder to yourself, which trickles into kindness shown to others. Your head is clear, and you intentionally do things in your day that matter. That's important. Sure, starting your day early takes a level of commitment, but the commitment is worth it.

For me, early means before 6:00 a.m. I know, I know—that's *early* early. As a wife, mom of three, and someone who works from home full-time, having uninterrupted me time is imperative but not easily attained. I have to wake up before my family every morning to do my best. Period. This is not the part where I tell you that you have to wake up at 5:00 a.m. to have a good and meaningful life. I wouldn't be telling you the truth. However, starting your day with things like silence, meditation, and prayer, when you relish both God's presence and your own, is an unmatched treat. Being still is meaningful because it allows you to simply *be*, instead of being in a routine of performative productivity. Being productive is cool. Being at peace is better. Finding peace early in the morning makes peace the official theme of the remainder of your day.

While rising at 5:00 or 6:00 a.m. may not be your style, I encourage you to start your day with at least fifteen minutes to yourself. Maybe that means waking at 7:15 before you have to share your time with your family, who normally wake at 7:30 a.m. I understand that getting out of bed is uncomfortable and inconvenient when you really want to sleep in or the day before was tough. You will have those days when sleeping in is more than fine. But if you can find a pocket of time—whether it's fifteen minutes or two hours—before saying anything to anybody, your mind and your heart will thank you for it.

That time is the difference between starting your day reactively and starting it proactively.

When you start your day **reactively**, you wake up to:

- A request from your spouse or kids that immediately affects your mood.
- Oversleeping and starting your day feeling frantic.
- Trying to remember everything that needs to get done today since you didn't plan and prep the day before.

When you start your day **proactively**, you wake up to:

- Feeling in control.
- Having time to prepare for what's to come for the day and going over your daily agenda.
- Having a quiet, peaceful beginning of the morning to yourself.

Some mornings will be inevitably reactive no matter how hard you try. But the beauty of being able to start your morning proactively is that you're setting the mood for the entire day. (Versus reactively, when other people or situations decide how the day will start for you.) Especially if you're not a morning person, you're probably wondering: "What am I supposed to do that early in the morning?" Well, this is a golden opportunity to come up with your own MAGIC morning routine. It doesn't have to be long or tedious—it just has to be meaningful to you. If it doesn't matter to you, if it's not something you look forward to, you won't wake up for it.

MAGIC MEMO

Decide when you want to wake up in the morning to spend uninterrupted time with yourself. There's no right or wrong time. Think about the natural rhythm of your household and how you can realistically get this done. Be honest with yourself. Whenever I had a newborn baby, no matter how badly I wanted to spend time with myself in the morning, 5:00 or even 6:00 a.m. proactive wake-ups were out of the question. Your wake-up time will look different in different seasons of your life. Once you decide the time, start by waking up fifteen minutes earlier than you did the morning before until you reach your ideal wake-up time. Let's say your goal wake-up time is 6:30 but you typically wake up at 7:45 a.m. Tomorrow morning, try waking up at 7:30, then the next morning 7:15, and so on until you reach your desired wake-up time of 6:30. If you miss your wake-up time, try again the following morning and the next until you're successful before moving on to an earlier time. While it's tempting to be ambitious and want to wake up at 5:00 every morning cold turkey, it's best to take it one day at a time so it becomes a habit and not a fluke. Apply that fifteen-minute rule to your bedtime as well. If you go to bed at 11:45 p.m., try 11:30 and so on until you're getting the sleep you need to wake up at your goal time.

Realistically, what time do you want to wake up in the morning? What will your MAGIC morning routine look like?

Why is spending time with yourself at the start of the day important to you?

If you want to have a stress-free day where you're ready for and confident to take on the day's tasks, get enough sleep and start your day early enough to spend meaningful time with yourself.

KNOWING WHY YOU'RE WAKING UP

Let's be clear, starting the day with yourself shouldn't be without purpose. To wake up before anyone else in your house, you want to know exactly what you will do when you wake up. You'll want to autopilot your morning as much as you can, so you don't have to make any SADs (small-ass decisions) in real time. When you do that, you often end up having decision fatigue before lunchtime. Free yourself and decide beforehand.

Why are you waking up early? Is it to have more time to read? To write? Quiet time because you talk to so many people for work or the kids have been extra energetic lately? For me, it's a little bit of all those things. And knowing what you will do during that extra quiet time is helpful to eliminate any chance of winging it that early in the morning. You can journal, meditate, work out, stretch, read, write, or just drink your coffee.

MAGIC BUT REAL

If you're not a morning person and don't have to deal with raising children, you have the luxury of starting your morning later. I encourage it. Productivity is not exclusive to the wee hours of the morning. However, even if you're not a morning person and you don't have small children, it typically benefits you to start the day with yourself proactively even if it means waking up a little bit earlier. It's a temporary discomfort with worthwhile results.

I'm always happy when I get the chance to drink a cup of coffee without having to microwave it for a third time before 8:00 a.m. When I wake up and start the day with myself intentionally, I get to do that.

If you're going to read, decide what you're going to read and make sure you put the book in the spot where you'll be reading. If you're going to journal, make sure you take the notebook and pen you're going to use and put them in the spot where you're going to sit and write. You can even decide what mug you're going to drink out of ahead of time and place it by the coffeemaker.

Those little ways of prepping for your morning make a noticeable difference and help to put your morning on autopilot. When there's not too much to think about, you can simply take it easy when you start your day. Most people don't start their day with themselves because they don't know what to do once they're up. Waking up proactively to spend time with yourself is meaningful—so decide what to do ahead of time. If you don't, it'll be too easy to hit the snooze button. When you know what you're going to do and prepare for it, your morning is simple and flows. Plus, you have something to look forward to the night before.

I try my best to wake up earlier than everyone else in my house. Some days are better than others. If I do wake up before everyone else, I have a peaceful morning routine and prepare myself for the day. I like water and coffee in the morning. I don't like to eat until around nine or ten. My body just feels better whenever I do that. My son wakes up at seven every single morning like he has to clock in at a morning job. So I'm mentally prepared for him to wake up at that time.

MAGIC MEMO

I like to say good morning to each of my kids (and Hubs) like I'm meeting Beyoncé. That always starts everyone off in a good mood for the day. When the first interaction your family has with you in the morning is a pleasant one, it's almost impossible to have a bad day. Always say, "Good morning." Always. Like my mom said to me growing up, "If we didn't sleep together last night, you've got to speak."

Mornings on the weekends look a little different, of course. On Saturdays, we have a big family breakfast, and on Sunday we have pastries or biscuits and head out to church. But we still say "Good morning" and start off being pleasant with one another.

In a few years, this will no longer be our season. The kids will be older and more independent and we'll have to readjust. We'll always be adjusting because change is both constant and inevitable. The reason for routines isn't to be perfect, but they do give us a sense of accomplishment. Routines often remind us that in fact we aren't perfect, but we are trying our best in the current season of our lives. That's really what it's all about—doing our best with what we have at the current moment.

THINKING TIME

One of my biggest motivators for waking up proactively before my family is so I can have thinking time. I know, you're likely wondering, "You need time to think, Mattie?" Yes, don't you? When everyone in my house wakes up it's go, go, go—nonstop—and then it's email, more email, Zoom meetings, and doing the work. Before all of that happens, I like to think without the interruption or influence of others.

This is a concept I discovered from *The Power of Focus*. In the book, coauthor Jack Canfield talks about discretionary time, which is time dedicated to focusing on whatever you want. You can focus on something personal or professional, and everyone around you knows that this time is for you to focus and to leave you be. This concept isn't exclusive—other books and thought leaders refer to it as CEO time. I like to treat it as thinking time. Realizing that you're more than enough requires thoughtfulness, and scheduling time to think gets you closer to that mindset.

Thinking time might be anywhere from five minutes to two hours. It's all based on your current needs for the day (or season) and how early you like to start your day. Don't underestimate your need to stop and think.

Here's another reason why thinking time is so important: we are taking in more information than any other generation in the history of time. Between emails, tweets, the endless scroll of our favorite social media platform, and the 24/7 news cycle, our brains rarely if ever get a break. So we have to schedule that break and allow our minds to think about what matters to us. It's tempting to be on the phone all the time. What makes uninterrupted morning thinking time so great is that it's usually so early that not much is going on. This encourages focus, clarity, and peace, which we could all use more of.

What could you use more clarity or focus on in this season?

Do you currently take time out to stop and think every day?

In your scheduled thinking time tomorrow, what do you want to think about?

You can approach thinking time however you see fit. I sit at the island in my kitchen with a notebook and write down my thoughts. Sometimes I write what's on my mind currently or I flesh out an idea I had the day before. The goal of thinking time is to have complete thoughts, uninterrupted. So, you guessed it, no phone. Thinking time is best utilized when you write out your thoughts in a notebook or in a word document on your computer. But anything that could potentially distract you—other people in person or online—should be shut down or off until thinking time is over.

Thinking time doesn't have to be long to be effective. When you're done with thinking time, even if it was only five minutes long, you'll feel refreshed and confident. Which means you can tackle the tasks of your day with a clear mind.

POCKETS OF PRODUCTIVITY

When people ask how I'm able to get so much done, I tell them it's because I look at lulls of time as POPs—pockets of productivity.

This is something that I learned from Jessica N. Turner's book *The Fringe Hours*. In the book, Jessica talks about how you can maximize your time when you're sitting in a car pool or in the waiting room at the doctor's office. Many times, we underestimate how much we can get done in fifteen to twenty minutes because it doesn't look like the two hours we'd like to have scheduled on our calendar.

The Fringe Hours was an eye-opening read because Turner discusses how a little bit of time is still valuable and useful in various seasons of life. POPs are about both life productivity and personal productivity. Sure, knocking things off your to-do list is useful on those days you're on a roll and have the capacity to do so. But after long stints of "knocking things out," you need to replenish and center yourself, which is also productive.

Instead of scrolling away on social media during the fifteen minutes you're waiting at the car wash, you can use a POP to finish a chapter of a book (pouring into yourself) or answer an email you put off earlier (producing results). It's about maximizing a pocket of time to be productive rather than allowing the time to just drain away.

POPs can be used every day. On the days you feel depleted, use your POPs to build yourself up and increase your personal productivity. On the days you have momentum, use your POPs to produce results and cross things off your to-do list. A POP is simply an intentional way to make your time MAGIC.

What are ways you can incorporate POPs into your day-to-day?

ROUTINES

We know routines are important and help maximize our time, but why? What is a routine? According to *Webster's* dictionary, a routine is a sequence of actions regularly followed; a fixed program. A routine is something you do every day for a specific reason. A bathtime routine is a series of actions you take to get everyone clean before bed. The bedtime routine is a series of actions you take to get everyone ready for bed.

The reset routine is to set the house up for success the next day.

Routines create rhythm in your home and life when you imple-ment them intentionally and apply them consistently. When you're clear on the reason you're doing something and why the routine actu-ally exists, you're more likely to use it consistently.

On the mornings when we're running late, it's usually because I skipped the reset routine the night before. In typical optimistic fash-ion, I kept telling myself, "No big deal. It won't take that long. We can still be on time." We had a fighting chance of being on time, but because I didn't reset the night before, it took us noticeably longer to get out the door. When that happens I'm instantly reminded of why we had established a routine in the first place.

OUR RESET ROUTINE

After dinner is such a great time to tidy up and get your home ready for the next day. This will look a little different for everyone, but creating a reset routine for your home allows you and your family to collectively prep your space for what the next day holds.

The reset routine is also powerful because it doesn't leave every-thing to one person. Your kids can help clear the table and load the dishwasher while your spouse takes out the trash. While that's hap-pening, you can make school lunches and take what's for dinner tomorrow out of the freezer to defrost. The possibilities are endless. And while you don't have to be Susie Homemaker or some domestic goddess to implement a reset routine, getting your space tidy to begin the next day is always a nice touch. No, this doesn't mean you need to wipe down the baseboards, but spending fifteen to thirty minutes clearing and wiping down counters, making sure there are no dishes in the kitchen sink, and making sure clothes and toys are off the floor and where they belong helps. Waking up to a house in order creates peace.

Remember, the reset routine is best carried out as a group activity; it's not something to do alone while resenting the rest of your family.

What would a reset routine look like for you?

Do you need to prep certain things the night before to ensure you have a calm evening or more productive morning the next day?

Is there a way you could get your family involved in the reset routine, so it doesn't all fall on you?

In your mind, what does a reset routine look like realistically?

BATH AND BEDTIME ROUTINES

We are not sticklers about much, but since my oldest was an infant, Chris has made sure that every night we have a bath and bedtime routine. Kids, like most people, respond well to consistency, and we try our very hardest to be consistent with our nighttime routines. Unless we're on vacation or stayed out later than originally planned, we always do bath and bedtime routines. What I've noticed is that when we don't do bath time and bedtime as usual, it's harder for the kids to fall asleep. And let me tell you something: Anything that helps my kids fall asleep *fast*, I am enthusiastically willing to do.

Because we're three kids in, it's no longer man-to-man coverage. Zone coverage means we have to divide and conquer. The girls are on a different schedule than our baby boy, so I bathe the girls in the kids' bathroom and Chris bathes our son in our bathtub. If we get an early enough start, I'll bathe the girls while the guys get playtime in the playroom. Then when we're done, Hubs will bathe Christian in the kids' bathroom.

I like to give the kids about ten minutes to play while I prepare their bedtime items. Prep is how I'm able to make this time aesthetically pleasing. While they're playing I put toothpaste on their toothbrushes, pull out their pajamas, and turn on soft lullaby music. Sometimes I even use a little lavender spray in their room to help encourage calmness. Again, if it helps them sleep and it's safe—I. Will. Do. It.

There's something very satisfying about seeing something prepared just for you. When you arrive at a hotel and the bed is made, toiletries neatly placed on the bathroom counters, and the fridge fully stocked—it's nice. It's nice to know that someone took the time out to prepare for you. I know my kids are little, but I like to make them feel like I took time out to prep their bedtime routine for them. Laying out their pajamas and placing their favorite stuffy on the bed to sleep with are just a couple of little ways to prepare them to have a good night. Sure, it takes me a few extra minutes to do that, but it's certainly worth it to me.

Is there a way you can prep a routine and make it aesthetically pleasing for yourself and your family?

Once they're out of the tub, the girls brush their teeth, and say their affirmations while looking in the mirror. Once we're done with affirmations, they get in their pajamas and then it's time for bed. The girls alternate each day and get to pick what we do for bedtime. My oldest loves what we call "talking time," and the middle one loves to read. If it's talking time, we set the timer for seven minutes and talk about whatever Maizah wants. If it's a reading night, then Caliana picks a book and we read it. (We're huge fans of the Pigeon books by Mo Willems. The girls can recite them verbatim.) Once we're done talking or reading (or sometimes both if they sucker me into it), I turn on sounds of the ocean for them and then we pray together. I let them each pray individually and then I pray over our family. Then it's lights-out.

Having a consistent and peaceful bedtime is one of the greatest things you can do for your children and yourself. It's not always the smoothest routine because kids have a mind of their own (and *lots* of energy). However, it's worth the effort.

My kids are just like your kids, I imagine—they ask for water, ask to use the bathroom, and make other random requests to delay bedtime a little more. I usually let them get away with a couple of delays and then I use my serious mom voice to reiterate that it's bedtime and that they need their rest. If it's a good night, it works. If not, we try to do what we can to get them to stay in bed. Sometimes that means the girls sleep together in one of their beds. Once they're asleep, Hubs usually puts the other sister in her own bed.

Have a set bedtime for yourself, just like you have a set wake-up time. Sure, hearing someone tell you that as an adult may seem ridiculous, but it's good advice. Set a bedtime and commit to it. Anytime you just wing it, and lie to yourself, thinking, *I'm an adult; I can go to bed late and still get it done tomorrow*, you usually end up paying for it the next day. Weekends and vacations are when you can give yourself grace, be a little bit more lenient, and go to bed and wake up later. But for the everyday, have a set bedtime.

And just like the kids do, you also want to have a bedtime routine.

Once the kids are down and things are prepped for tomorrow, set your alarm for when you would like to get up. Depending on the season and your workload, give yourself the time you need. If you want to get some extra rest, set your alarm later. Having a peaceful alarm sound will also allow you to start your day off on the right foot. Can we agree to stop letting the phone make us jump out of our sleep because the alarm sound is so jarring? That is just not the way you want to wake up and start your day. We jump out of our sleep and wonder why we're stressed or in a bad mood in the morning. Once I started choosing more pleasant alarm sounds, I started my days off so much more peacefully. If you have an iPhone, try sounds like Rise or Chimes as they gradually get louder and maintain a peaceful, rhythmic sound to wake you up. (Also, when your alarm sounds are annoying, you're more likely to slam the snooze button instead of just waking up.)

SCREEN TIME ROUTINES

Because I create online content for a living, I'm on my phone a lot and I have to set some boundaries so I stay sane and don't experience burnout. I hate burnout. I repeat, I hate burnout, and I will set whatever boundaries are necessary to avoid it. I believe in working hard, but not at the cost of my peace and well-being.

Your phone can be such a time suck. Set a social media or phone curfew for yourself to create some healthy boundaries at night. (Some nights will be better than others.) We do a twenty-four-hour screen fast as a family every week, but I give myself a 9:30 p.m. phone curfew to give my brain a break from the endless scroll of comments, opinions, and the 24/7 news cycle. Sometimes I do use my phone to watch TV or a movie while I'm in the bath. So, it's not always a complete phone curfew, but I'm okay with that.

Of course, at the end of the day, there's your nighttime skin-care routine, which we discussed earlier. Take the time to enjoy this process because it is another opportunity for you time. It's a therapeutic process that requires you to be present and intentional. Your nighttime skin-care routine doesn't have to be fancy or elaborate to matter. Mine is, but that's because I really enjoy the process. It's all about using products that make your skin look and feel good. Even on your laziest and most exhausted nights, remove your makeup. NEVER EVER SLEEP WITH MAKEUP ON. As much of an effort as that may take, you're worth the effort, and waking up with clean skin is always worth it.

Everyone's different, but I like taking a bath or shower at night to wash off the day. If I can get away with it, I will take a bath every single night. (I didn't have a bathtub in my old house that we lived in for ten years, so I'm making up for lost time.) It's a little way of indulging every day and really helps you decompress. If baths aren't your thing or you don't have one, you can take really nice showers with a bodywash you enjoy or even add a shower bomb from the drugstore or Amazon. They are glorious. While bathing is a routine task you do every day, making it your own and allowing yourself to add a little MAGIC is worth the effort.

How can you make your bath or shower at night more enjoyable?

What products do you enjoy at bath time that you'd like to incorporate more of into your routine?

Last but not least is putting on your "sleep clothes" as my mom and grandma used to say. To know me is to know I take pajamas seriously. I'm a firm believer that how you look can contribute to how you feel, so I wear pajamas that make me look and feel good. This doesn't have to be an expensive feat by any means. Some of my favorite pairs are from Target and Amazon. Pajamas are part of your sleep wardrobe. If you like matching sets, find a set you love (and buy it in more than one color if your budget allows). If you love sleeping in T-shirts you've gotten from concerts, build a collection and rotate them. If negligees are your speed, indulge in wearing them to sleep. If sleeping in organic cotton sweats tickles your fancy, I support that too. The goal here is to sleep in what makes you feel good and comfortable when you go to bed. I believe what you wear contributes to your confidence and many of us are not going to sleep feeling confident. Tired? Exhausted? Stressed? Yes. But confident? When's the last time you went to bed feeling confident about yourself and ready for the morning?

In my opinion, pajamas matter because they're our outfit for bed. Love a certain cartoon character? Over-the-top? (Raises hand.) Laid-back? There are pajamas for all of us, no matter our personality type. There's something magical that happens to us when we slip into a set of pajamas and look put together for bed. It's the effort of having some sort of order when we go to sleep that gives us confidence for the morning.

Once my pajamas are on, it's time for bed. Setting the mood to have a peaceful sleep is worth the effort. It's also a sure way to guarantee I'll wake up on the right foot to have a MAGIC morning.

Your time is just that—it's yours. Planning to enjoy your time by making your mornings MAGIC, having thinking time, maximizing your POPs throughout the day, and intentionally and consistently having routines that set you and your family up for success all allow you to enjoy your time for the gift it is.

CHAPTER SEVEN

The MAGIC of Things

*Every day is better when you
keep your things in order.*

I imagine you like your things. You should, they're yours. But then there's your kids' things as well. Outside of household items, there's all your clothes and shoes and then your kids' clothes and shoes. And toys. And books. And artwork. It can be a lot, especially if you're not sure how to organize and manage those things. What do you purge? What do you keep? And if you keep it, where does it go?

There's nothing wrong with having things because there are uses for things. And when you manage them, things have MAGIC. If they don't, that is when you want to get rid of them.

The MAGIC of things is that they can bring you joy. There are meaningful items—be it toys or clothes—that you deem aesthetically pleasing and your goal is to intentionally and consistently take care of them, so they continue to bring you and your family joy. Whether you're a frugal Fran like my bestie is or bougie like me, your things matter, and they can make MAGIC when managed properly.

My husband and I met on Myspace (shout-out to Tom). Yes, true story. He messaged me and after months of keeping in touch on almost a daily basis, we met one day at the mall where I worked. Years later, after getting married, I asked him what made him reach out to me. Naturally, I was hoping for an answer like "I thought you were pretty" or "You looked good." His reply: "You looked like a lot of fun." At the moment, I have to admit I didn't like that answer.

Now? I love it.

Wearing clothes that let me have fun and be myself makes me happy. It really does. I'm an over-the-top extrovert who will wear a dress to almost any occasion. Church, dropping my kids off at school, lunch with my girlfriends, a football game—you name it. I am going to wear what lets me have fun and what makes me feel confident and most like me. I wasn't always this way.

When I first started creating online content, my budget was modest, so I thrifted everything. Honestly, I loved this stage because it really allowed me to learn about silhouettes and how clothes were made years ago. It also challenged me to lean into what I actually liked.

Then I went through a phase of trying to follow all of the popular trends I saw on Pinterest and Instagram. I tried to copy my favorite influencers and it girls—but I'd fall short because of a low budget and a lack of authenticity. It was short-lived, but I even went through that dreaded wear-nothing-but-neutral-colors phase. Looking back, it was laughable. There was nothing wrong with that, but it just wasn't and isn't me.

When it comes to your personal style, it's supposed to change. Because you're allowed to change—to grow and evolve. That growth and those changes will inevitably be reflected in your wardrobe.

Currently in my life, I'm in a place where my wardrobe is deliberately feminine, willingly fun, and noticeably authentic. I'm not trying to look like anyone but my truest self.

That should be the goal with your personal style—looking and feeling like your truest, most confident self. Anything you wear that doesn't make you feel like this is a complete disservice to you. I believe we should dress to express ourselves, not to impress others. This requires us to be explicitly honest with ourselves. I've learned that editing my closet, discovering my MAGIC uniform, and having trusted wardrobe pieces that never fail me and come through in clutch moments all help me dress with confidence.

EDITING YOUR CLOSET

Let me say this: your personal style is a form of self-care. While we touched on self-care in an earlier chapter, it was important to me to make personal style its own section. I get questions daily from women, especially new moms, asking how they find their own personal style after having kids. I totally get it. When big changes happen in our lives—having a baby, graduating, moving cross-country, getting a new job—our confidence is often more delicate than usual. How you dress is a protective shield from the outside world that often tries to dilute your confidence.

Your personal style can be MAGIC—yes, it can be meaningful, aesthetically pleasing, goal-oriented, intentional, and consistent. We all have our "I'm in sweatpants all day today" moments, but going out of your way to build a wardrobe that makes you feel your best is important.

I recently had lunch with one of my girlfriends whom I adore and respect. She's a rock star of a mother, a bestselling author, and one of the most incredible entrepreneurs I've ever met. She complimented me on my dress and stated, "I've been buying more dresses lately and I really want to wear them, but I always think, *Why? I'm just at home. Is it worth the hassle?*"

I replied, "Even if you're just at home, aren't you worth the effort? You're worth the hassle. We go through the hassle for our families and businesses, why not ourselves?"

If loungewear is what makes you feel relaxed, laid-back, and confident, wear it. If dresses and fancy tops make you feel like your most confident self? Wear them. Yes, even if it does take extra time and effort. You are always worth the time and effort. So is the confidence you gain when you put on what you want and commit.

I love a good closet declutter. It is time-consuming and a lot of effort—but it's worth it. You end up creating space and organizing your closet in a way that gets you excited about getting dressed. Here's how to edit your closet.

What you must know is that this is a task that will take time and commitment. Without question, editing your closet, depending on how many clothes you have, will likely take you anywhere from two to six hours to complete.

First, pull everything out of your closet. Yep, every single thing. If you have drawers in your closet, empty those out as well.

Then, in Marie Kondo style, go through every single piece and audit it.

Does it bring you joy?

Does it fit?

Do you wear it? Not *would* you wear it, but DO YOU wear it?

If you answer no to any of these questions, toss it to the side to later (1) pass on, (2) donate, or (3) trash.

After you audit your closet, you'll want to organize it.

A couple of years ago, I had the good fortune of having the wonderful team from *The Home Edit* virtually organize my closet. And yes, they are that *good*. (Even virtually.) After having my closet organized, I started looking at my closet as a wardrobe map of sorts.

The purpose of your wardrobe map is to give you direction on what to wear. To simplify how to navigate that map, I organized my closet by color, type, and length.

What I learned from *The Home Edit* team is the power and resourcefulness of ROYGBIV. Color-coding your closet helps you find whatever you need quickly and easily. But if ROYGBIV isn't your thing because you have more neutral-toned clothing, you can still organize tonally going from light to dark.

A guide for if you choose to organize ROYGBIV:

- Red
- Orange
- Yellow
- Green
- Blue
- Purple
- Pink
- White
- Brown
- Gray
- Black

A guide for if you choose to organize from light to dark to vibrant:

- White
- Cream
- Beige
- Khaki
- Brown
- Black
- Gray
- Pink
- ROYGBIV

Now that you've organized your wardrobe by color, you can section it off by type, length, and weight. You want to keep each section color-coded, but the sections themselves will help you find specific pieces easily.

A guide for sections in your closet (hanging):

- Blazers
- Blouses/Shirts/Tops
- Dresses
- Pants/Trousers
- Outerwear (Coats and Jackets)

A guide for sections in your closet (drawers and shelves):

- Bras and Underwear
- Denim
- Sweaters
- Pajamas
- Loungewear
- Swimwear
- Accessories
- Shoes

When it comes to your wardrobe on hangers, start with length then weight. For instance, with the tops section, keep all the same color together. Then organize the section starting with your short-sleeved tops then long-sleeved until you get to another color. If you have many white short-sleeved tops, start with the lightest material and progress to the heaviest material. A linen blouse starts the section while a knit top ends it.

Organizing by color, sectioning by type, and segmenting by weight will allow you to find pieces in your closet quickly.

MAGIC MEMO

Also rid your closet of anything that's stained, torn, or damaged in any way. Unless you know how to get the stain out or sew up the tear or hole, it likely isn't worth keeping. Sure, there are exceptions—like something of sentimental value or even a luxury/vintage piece. But likely, this thing you're holding on to has been waiting to be thrown away.

CLOTHES THAT FIT

One thing that will absolutely make you feel confident no matter what you wear is making sure your clothes fit.

I have heard so many women in my life (myself included) say, "I'm [keeping/buying/saving] this for when I lose weight." How many times have you made this wild statement to yourself?

Not sure about you (because we're all different), but when I wear clothes that don't fit—particularly clothes that are too small for me— it does not make me feel good. And it also doesn't make sense to pressure myself to become this "ideal" size before I can wear something I really want to.

Here's what I want you to know: if you've gained weight, you're still worthy of wearing clothes that make you feel amazing and confident.

If you've lost weight, you're still worthy of wearing clothes that make you feel amazing and confident.

Editing your closet isn't about having a lot of clothes—it's about having pieces that fit, represent who you are, and make you feel great.

Many times, when it comes to the clothes we want to wear, we think we have a weight issue when it's really a fit issue. A size 2 is just as wonderful as a size 24, especially when you dress accordingly.

Many of us make the mistake of keeping or buying clothes that don't fit and as a result we feel "less than" and wish we were something we're currently not. Unless the clothes have actual sentimental value to you (a wedding dress, your first luxury piece, etc.), if they don't fit—get rid of them.

Pass the clothing or item on to a relative or friend who can fit into it, donate it to an organization that matters to you, or trash it. But hanging on to it because one day you might fit in it again is a waste of time and closet space.

MAGIC BUT REAL

For the longest time, I kept an item in my closet that didn't fit—a pair of my premom jeans. These were jeans I could fit into before having any of my babies. I had this wild daydream that one day, after getting really consistent with working out and eating healthy, I'd be back to my prebaby weight. The thing is, I don't even want to get back to my prebaby weight. I just want to feel energetic and strong while looking good in my clothes. It was only a few months ago that I finally let go of my premom jeans. And it was a weight lifted. No regrets. Not sure who this is for, but you can let go of the "premom" you. "Mom" you is worthy of your MAGIC wardrobe—yep, even with a different body. Here's the thing—even if you do ever get back to your prebaby or goal weight, you can just buy new jeans instead of holding on to old ones.

YOUR MAGIC UNIFORM

Okay, so now you can see everything in your closet and everything in it fits! You put in a lot of work to get to this point, so bravo! Now, let's determine your MAGIC wardrobe.

Let's do a quick exercise. Grab a pen and paper or even your phone—yes, right now—and sit down comfortably in a place where you can take some brief notes.

I want you to close your eyes and imagine yourself—your current self—in your closet getting ready for the day. It's a regular day, nothing out of the usual is going to happen. If you could pick any outfit to wear to feel like your most confident self, what would it be? Visualize it. Can you see yourself in this look? Imagine what it feels like to have it on. You look good, right? Take a deep breath before you open your eyes. Open them slowly after visualizing.

Write down exactly what you wore and how it made you feel.

When you visualized yourself, how did you feel?

Confident?

Powerful?

Capable?

Fun?

Were you wearing...

A dress?

A blazer?

Jeans and a T-shirt?

Really fancy loungewear?

What color were the clothes?

Light colors? Bright colors? Neutrals?

How about silhouette or shape?

Were there any prints or patterns?

Were you wearing accessories? Jewelry? A hat? Sunglasses?

This ideal outfit you've visualized is what I call your MAGIC uniform. For me, I'd absolutely be wearing a floral print dress with statement heels and bright-colored lipstick. That's what makes me feel confident. My favorite thing about this exercise is that there are no right or wrong answers here.

Now that you've envisioned your MAGIC uniform, your job is to try to incorporate a little of it into your everyday wardrobe.

If you visualize yourself wearing bright colors, wear some bright colors daily—even if it's only your earrings or lipstick. If you were wearing a great pair of denims, wear jeans with a variety of tops that make you feel great. Your subconscious just gave you your MAGIC dress code. It's your job to make it a reality a little bit every day. If your wardrobe allows you to, you can emulate exactly what you visualized in different ways day to day. If you follow me on Instagram, you'll see that I wear a dress 80 percent of the time. It just makes me feel like me. And I want you to dress like you—your best YOU—every day.

WARDROBE STAPLES

I'll be the first one to tell you that I don't believe in most of the wardrobe rules. I believe in wearing black with brown and silver with gold and even jeans with a dress. Most of those rules are outdated and the truth is, confidence can make anything look good. Here's also what makes you confident about your wardrobe: having pieces in your closet that just work. In addition to your MAGIC uniform, the following seven pieces serve most women in a variety of looks. This is not a rule by any means, but more of a guide. Take what you need; leave what you don't.

The Go-To Blazer

Once upon a time, the black blazer was the piece every editor from every fashion blog and magazine believed you had to have. I sort of agree with this. I believe you need a blazer in your wardrobe—it just doesn't have to be black. I have a black blazer—one from H&M—that has yet to fail me, and to this day it's the best $70 I've spent in that store. However, I also have a red one from ZARA with gold buttons that fits like it was made for me. (Fun fact: my sister, Maya, and I bought this same blazer without knowing and wore it on the same day.) I truly believe that having at least one go-to blazer in your preferred color will elevate your wardrobe.

Works-with-My-Shape Midi Dress

Midi dresses are my best friend. (Sorry, Erica.) I love their versatility and how they make me look. A midi dress is a dress that falls at least two inches below the knees but stays above the ankles. Basically, it's longer than a minidress but shorter than a maxi dress. Midi dresses work in every season and for every body type. If you're short—they work. If you're tall—they still work. They go with sandals, pumps, booties, and boots. And there's a variety of silhouettes—sheath, body con, A-line, and more. It's all about finding the silhouette that works for your shape.

Wear-with-Anything Flats or Sneakers

While I live for heels, I do believe in versatile flats or sneakers for the sake of being practical. (Only a little bit.) Flats have the ability to be super chic, whether you opt for a ballet flat, espadrille, or loafer mule. (I still swear by the Gucci Princetown mules.) And you cannot underestimate a great pair of sneakers. One of my favorite looks on women is a super-girly or frilly dress with a fly pair of sneakers. (I will never tire of the Jordan 4's. NEVER.) "Flats are boring" is a lie. You just have to find the ones that work for you.

Button-Up Shirt

This is likely not the first time you're hearing that if you have one good piece in your closet, it should be a button-up shirt. That's for good reason. It is undefeated. It is versatile enough to go with denim, under sweaters and vests, and still pairs beautifully with a blazer. It just works. Now, long gone are the days where you should own only a white one. If a crisp white button-up does it for you, by all means have at it. But don't think it needs to be fitted or white to give you options. I live for an oversized "Dad shirt" version in a soft pastel or even pinstripes. It looks good tucked into your perfect-fit jeans or tied up over a dress or with a skirt.

Power Heels

At the risk of forcing you to wear heels if you don't, I think we all need a pair of power heels that make us feel unstoppable. You've got an extra pep in your step when you wear them. In fact, when you wear them you don't even walk—you strut. They're that good. Power heels look good with jeans, dresses, and, really, any piece of clothing you own. Depending on your preference and the season, they can be pumps, boots, or sandals. A couple of years ago, I splurged and bought the blue Manolo pumps that Carrie wore in the first *Sex and the City* movie. Not only do they go with almost anything in my closet, but they always make me feel amazing when I wear them.

The Statement Accessory

Jewelry is so fun. My girls love to come into my closet and play with earrings and rings. And there's nothing quite like a statement piece of jewelry to pull a simple look together and make it pop. Whether it's an oversized chain-link necklace or emerald chandelier earrings, the statement accessory is a conversation starter that, in my opinion, adds an extra layer of confidence to your look. If it were an Infinity Stone, it would be the Confidence Stone. Your statement accessory doesn't have to be expensive either. I just recently purchased the most beautiful green resin chandelier earrings for $45. It's impossible to ignore them and they go with everything.

Perfect-Fit Jeans

Finding the right jeans is quite the task. You'll probably have to go through quite a few pairs of jeans to figure out what cut best complements your body, what wash you prefer, and what size you take in certain brands (you'd be surprised how varied denim sizing can be). I'll tell you what, though, it is absolutely worth the hassle. Because when you find a pair of jeans that fit you absolutely perfectly, it is a breath of fresh air in your wardrobe. In fact, when I found my perfect-fit jeans, I bought them in two different washes to have options throughout the year. Jeans are fantastic, of course, because they go with so many different things. You can dress them up with heels and a pretty blouse or dress them down with sneakers and a statement tee. The possibilities are endless, especially when you have a pair with the perfect fit for you.

You don't have to be a fashionista to dress in a way that makes you feel confident and beautiful. You simply have to be intentional about finding what works for you. With an edited closet—filled with clothes that fit and reliable pieces that work—you can set yourself up to dress for confidence.

CLOTHES-MINDED

When it comes to clothes and what they prefer to wear, all of my kids are different but very opinionated. Maizah loves separates and statement pieces. Caliana is very much my princess and would wear a dress every day. Christian wants comfort—anything that is even the slightest fuss, he's out.

I know how much clothes contribute to my confidence as an adult and so I try to keep that in mind with my kids too. As long as it's weather- and age-appropriate, I let the kids pick what they want to wear. Not only do I think that helps contribute to their decision-making skills, but I truly believe it gives them a sense of self. At home, we don't have "good clothes" that our kids need to save until a special moment. If one wants to wear a sequined jacket today, by all means, do so.

I did not grow up like this at all. There were special clothes for church and going out with my parents. The "regular clothes" I could wear to school. However, I do remember my mom dressing me up in a girly and frilly dress for school pictures in second grade. The dress was peach and white, and on the bodice part there was some sort of sequined embellishment. I wanted to wear my hair in one puff with a bow. I also had an attachment to a really sporty digital watch. To the point that I refused to take it off for pictures. But I do remember that my mom said it was okay to keep it on if I wanted to. She didn't try to convince me otherwise and lo and behold, that watch was very prominent in my school picture. However, my mom giving me space to choose how I styled my hair and chose my accessories truly did shape how I viewed myself. I had the power to pick what I liked.

I try to give my kids that same power with their clothes.

As far as organizing clothes is concerned, we either fold them or hang them. I believe in file-folding so we can find things easily. As we discussed in chapter 3, file-folding is when you take a piece— T-shirt, jeans, skirt, for example—trifold it (fold it over twice into three folds), and stand it up in the drawer like a file. By doing this instead of setting the clothes on top of each other, you can take inventory and select what you want to wear faster.

We hang items like noncotton or formal dresses, dress shirts, suits, blazers, and jumpsuits. I like to reserve drawers for more casual and durable pieces. I purchased a couple of fifty-packs of velvet kid hangers in different colors. As I mentioned earlier, Maizah's are pink, Caliana's are purple, and Christian's are gray, which pretty much matches their bedroom colors. And it automates a SAD—once I see a color, I know exactly whose clothes should be hung on it.

PURGING THE OLD STUFF

I've started the habit of clearing things out every quarter so we can stay sane. Having stuff is nice. Having so much stuff that it overwhelms you is not. I don't want my kids to have that feeling, and including them in the process when they're old enough is practical. They not only get to help you purge, but they learn that letting go of stuff is a good thing and putting in the effort to purge is worth it.

Similar to the process for purging your own closet, get rid of anything that doesn't fit, or has an unfixable hole or stain on it. Take a Saturday morning or a Get-It-Done day and have at it. Put on a music playlist and knock it out together in an hour or two. Toss everything that's no good in a contractor trash bag and toss it.

Toys, Books, and Artwork

Toys, books, and artwork will take you out unless you have a dedicated space for playing and reading. We have a playroom, but even having a play corner will give you peace of mind. It lets you and your kiddos know that this is the designated space for toys and stuff. There comes a point when we start having too many toys and books for the designated play space…simply put, we have too much. I elaborate on this in chapter 3, but I'll give you the trailer version here. If the toys and artwork are taking over the space where they are to be kept, then it's time to edit and purge.

First things first, there must be a designated place for everything. The more specific, the better. Also, having a designated time when the kids—yes, those cute freeloaders who live with you rent-free—clean up the space. I'm not a chore sergeant by any means, but every Saturday all of my kids (yes, even the small one for five minutes) clean the playroom before they are allowed to begin play for the day. It gives them a sense of responsibility and teaches them how to work together.

Storage will be your very best friend. A lot of the time we do in fact have the space for toys and other things, but we don't have the storage. Take a solid inventory of what your kids play with: How big are the toys? Do they have more than one of the same type of toy?

Does the play area have space for storage? Would tall storage or wide storage work better?

We have everything from LEGO sets, Barbies, and stuffed animals to crayons, construction paper, and all types of Disney toys in the kids' playroom. A couple of years ago when we moved into our home, we had no toy storage. While one of those fancy-schmancy playroom toy storage walls was out of our budget at the time, I had to get creative or the toys were going to take over. Here are some really great toy and artwork storage ideas:

- Baskets
- Hampers
- Bins
- Three-tiered carts
- Bowls
- Cups
- Cubbies
- Binders
- Jars
- Drawers

We have an eight-cube cubby storage in the kids' playroom and it is a godsend. In the top four cubes we store books that are not in active rotation (the books we do read regularly are in their bedroom on a floating shelf). When they want to switch up the rotation, they know they have to trade a book for a book. To make the books in their playroom cubby aesthetically pleasing, we've organized them in

ROYGBIV order. When the kids clean up, it gives them a simple way to remember what order the books go in.

In the bottom four cubes in the cubby storage, we have baskets I got from Hobby Lobby that fit almost perfectly. The first two baskets are for LEGOs. All. Of. The. LEGOs. There are so many. So when it comes to tidying up, if it's a LEGO brick, it goes in one of these two baskets. The other two baskets are for small random toys that don't belong to a set and Barbie dolls.

MAGIC MEMO

We have a rule in the house about toys: if it's small enough for you to swallow, it gets tossed. Honestly, there are enough things to be stressed about as a parent; the kids choking on a toy shouldn't be one of them. It's a rule in place until all of my kids are older than five, and then hopefully it won't even be an issue. You're probably thinking there are so many toys that are small enough to swallow, especially in toy sets. You're right. I throw them ALL away. So if Barbie's dog is a supersmall toy that the baby could potentially swallow, Barbie no longer has a dog. I'm flexible in a lot of areas. This isn't one of them.

Here's what has been clutch for holding most of my kids' medium-sized and larger toys—laundry hampers. I found a three-basket hamper at Walmart a few years ago, and it has been a saving grace. We pushed it to the limit recently and one of the baskets tore (it's three linen baskets held by metal rods), so I just ordered a replacement. Best $30 I've spent for the playroom—easily. Because hampers are tall and deep, they make great storage for bigger toys that are an awkward shape. Even adding a couple of these in your kids' play area will eliminate much of the toy clutter.

For artwork, I took a page out of my friend Kendra's book—no, literally, she wrote a series of books titled *The Lazy Genius*. She has a designated bin for her kids' artwork. When it gets full, they go through and keep the most meaningful ones and toss the rest. We have a drawer for this. In the kids' playroom, we have an eight-drawer organizer. This is where we store paper, crayons, colored pencils, and markers. Each of the kids has an artwork drawer. When the drawer is full, we go through and let them pick the ones that actually matter. I keep the meaningful ones in a binder in sheet protectors. When the binder gets full, we make a book out of all the artwork and keep the book as a memento for the kids when they get older.

MAGIC BUT REAL

For now, oversized toys get neatly placed in a corner or against the wall until I come up with something better. That's all I got.

A KID'S PLACE

Growing up I moved around *a lot*. The CliffsNotes version of it: I was born in Huntsville, Alabama, on a business trip; spent the first two years of my life in Toronto; went to preschool in Saudi Arabia; and moved back to Huntsville for kindergarten and first grade. Then, during my second through fourth grades, we lived in Atlanta; then Philadelphia, where we moved twice; and I went to three different schools for fifth through eighth grades. I did all of high school right outside of Pittsburgh in a small town called Beaver. Being the new kid who usually was the token Black kid, with immigrant parents, was more than I realized back then. And so my bedroom was sacred. It was a space I could call my own, especially when I got to the tenth grade and I no longer had to share with my sister, Maya.

Having a space where I could read books and magazines I loved, run my mouth on the phone with my friends, and listen to music was a treat. We don't move as much as I did when I was a kid, but I wanted to make sure that I gave my kids a space for them to enjoy and where they felt free to be themselves.

Chris and I really enjoy decorating our kids' bedrooms. The girls share a room and Christian has his own room. Whether shared or solo, we knew that we wanted to personalize their rooms to feel like places where they belonged. To make a kid's room their PLACE, you want it to have:

Personalization
Light

Access

Color

Energy

Personalization

In the girls' room, we purchased oversized wooden letters of the first initial in each of their names, and Chris painted them white. We hung them over their beds to sort of mark their territory. In Christian's room, Chris made a beautiful framed art piece with wallpaper and his first initial. We also have a handful of framed photos of each of them in the rooms. Kids being able to see themselves is important.

Light

Christian hit the jackpot. Baby boy has three windows in his nursery, giving him the most daylight of any room in the house. I honestly believe that's why he has such a sunny disposition. We also have a floor lamp for lower light during bedtime and a flush mount on the ceiling light. The girls have only one window, but because of where it's placed, they get a lot of daylight in their bedroom as well. Outside of the ceiling light, we have a small lamp on their dresser to provide lower light in the evening.

Access

It's important for the kids to have access to whatever they might need. Sure, I'm all about decor and order, but I want their rooms to be just as functional as they are beautiful. For the girls, we chose a dresser that made it possible for them to reach all the drawers, and there's a stool in their closet. And while they have books in their playroom, we keep five or six books on clear Montessori floating shelves at each of their bedsides. They can easily access whatever they'd like to read. In Christian's room, there's a small bookshelf for his books. We face them out—Montessori-style—so he can grab whatever book he'd like.

Color

The girls' beds are positioned on each side of the room with a window in the middle. We found two curtain panels to match their favorite colors and painted the walls that their beds sit next to in their respective favorite colors. Caliana's side is lavender and Maizah's is mint green. We've kept the theme consistent—if it's in their room, Cali gets lavender and Maizah gets mint. For Christian's room, we opted for a soft gray and denim blue as his colors. I think all the kids' colors have a vibrance yet softness that promotes joy and peace.

Energy

Speaking of joy and peace, that's exactly the kind of energy we want not only in our rooms, but also in their rooms. I want them to have a place where they can decompress if they've had a bad day. A place where they can be vulnerable with us as a family and a place where they feel safe. A place where they can get tickled, get surprised on the morning of their birthdays, a place where they say their prayers at night. A place for kids.

A kid's PLACE is a place that feels like their own.

Having things and taking care of them isn't about performative materialism when you understand why they make MAGIC in your life. The clothes in your life can make you feel amazing, while organizing the kids' toys can get them excited about playing with them again. Keeping and having things that are meaningful to you matters. They often make you feel beautiful and create goals of intentionality and consistency within your life and home. It doesn't get more MAGIC than that.

CHAPTER EIGHT

Making Your Memories MAGIC

"Remember the time..."

When I turned sixteen, we lived right outside Pittsburgh, Pennyslvania, and on one Memorial Day weekend, we drove to Columbus, Ohio, to visit my uncle Fred and his family. My birthday always ends up falling on Memorial Day weekend and my parents didn't really consider that their sixteen-year-old might want to do something with her friends that weekend. I was super annoyed—so much so that I didn't get dressed at all that weekend. I had my headscarf on the day of my birthday, and when they surprised me with a cake, I was not really photo-ready. But my dad being my dad, he insisted that we get photos. And now, whenever I look at photos of my "sweet 16," I get to see myself in all my awkward adolescent glory wearing a headscarf.

If my dad is good at anything, he's good at making sure we get a picture together as a family. He's always been that way. As a hormonal sixteen-year-old, it was sometimes annoying because he would encourage me to smile when I didn't want to take a photo during big moments, but now, looking back, I'm so glad he did. Yep, even wearing sweats and a head wrap.

My mom has done an incredible job of taking and storing photos of us as kids and even other relatives. As the first American generation in a Liberian family, I have quite a few relatives I haven't met or met only when I was under the age of four and don't remember. However, my mom can reference back to old photo albums that she's kept and show us our aunts, uncles, cousins, grandparents, and even great-grandparents thanks to photos. That is so special to me. And if we take care of them like my mom has, I'll get to show those same photos to my kids, so they can see photos of relatives in their family tree whom they may likely never meet.

Seeing relatives and family members who mean so much to me, my sister, and my parents, is sentimental to me because of all the stories and memories shared. Both my parents have amazing stories of growing up—my mom is the second-oldest of six girls and grew up on a rubber tree farm. My dad, the oldest of nine, graduated high school at fifteen and was the first in his family to go to college, which he did on a full scholarship at University of Liberia. Their stories about how they met, about the friends they made and stayed close with even once they moved to the States, are tales I'll never forget because those events shaped who they have become.

My parents moved to the United States in 1980 and let me tell you, just the hairstyles and fashions in their photos from those times are gems, even without any backstory. I don't know about you, but seeing my parents when they were young people is one of my favorite things. Even seeing myself or my sister as a kid tickles me. Having photo evidence of the people you love—who they were, what they did, and where they were—is an irreplaceable treat.

Remembering the time with loved ones and my own personal experiences is so special to me. That's why it's a priority to me to capture moments with my family and throughout my life to reference back to as I grow older.

I like being in photos—luckily, that's worked out for me as an influencer—and I love how they allow you to freeze a moment in time so you can save that memory.

I absolutely love pictures. I love photos so much that I have 67,874 photos in my camera roll on my iPhone. I even opted out of having a videographer at my wedding. I know myself. I would never just sit there and watch the video more than once or twice. But photos? I'll look at them all the time, reminiscing about the day and my favorite moments.

Your memories as a family are MAGIC. And thanks to smartphones, we now have professional-quality cameras with ample cloud storage to save all of our photos and even videos. While I am a digital photo kind of girl, having physical copies of photos (framed and in photo books), organizing photos of the kids for future reference, and taking one good family photo every year are things I have recently started prioritizing. The kids are growing fast, so many awesome life changes are happening, and I want to remember these times. I am by no means an expert when it comes to the organization of photos, but here's what's working for me.

ORGANIZING FAMILY PHOTOS IN YOUR PHONE

We all have an obnoxious amount of photos on our phones, especially if we have kids. However, most of us won't print these out and aren't saving these to a hard drive or the cloud. Here's what I urge you to do sooner rather than later: organize the photos and videos on your phone by family members. Right now, I have a folder for myself, a folder for Chris, and a folder for each of the kids. I even have a folder for our group shots and one for photos of the kids together without us. I have to admit, sitting down as a family and looking at photos is beautiful because you get to hear everyone's perspective from that experience. You can redo some moments if you decide it could've been better or even repeat what was a hit for everyone. We take in quite a lot of information day to day thanks to email, social media, and our things-to-do lists. Photos allow you to escape and remember a fun moment you might have briefly forgotten about.

Photos of my family are meaningful to me. And while I have an obnoxious number of photos, I believe organizing photos in a way that lets me reference them later—like when I want to find pictures of certain holidays or special occasions—matters. Once a week or so (if I remember to set a reminder), I go through my camera roll and save photos to their respective folders. The folders of my family members are a shared folder, so both Chris and I can upload to them, depending on who recently took photos. My best friend and I also share a folder with photos of our oldest daughters, who are best friends. That way when they have playdates or moments at school together, we can upload so we all have access to the photos, no matter who took them.

Shared folders are great especially when you have relatives you're close with who don't live close by. Sure, they can see the pictures on social media, but not everyone is on social media—especially older relatives. Also, there might be photos of some moments that you'd like to reserve for only your family instead of posting on a public platform. (Such as the birth of a new child, an announcement of pregnancy, the purchase of a new home, where you're traveling, etc.) Loved ones always feel appreciated when you share a photo of a special moment with them via text or email. I know I certainly do.

The great thing about photos is that they don't have to be professionally captured to be meaningful. It's simply about having them. Once you've organized photos in your phone, you can easily access them for future reference.

FAMILY PHOTO ARCHIVES

My sister is certainly like my dad when it comes to taking photos. She always remembers to capture us in the moment or isn't afraid to ask the stranger at the table next to us at brunch to take our picture.

She's also been consistently warning me to make sure I create folders and storage for the kids to access all their photos when they get older. She's absolutely right.

Well, if it isn't the bridge I said I'd cross when I got there—storage for all my kids' photos. A month or so ago, I created a Google Drive folder for all our family photos. Similar to the method I used to organize them on my phone, I've designated a folder for each family member, group shots of all of us, and group shots of just the kids. Within each of these folders, I've created year subfolders—starting with the year each kid was born. For Chris and me, I created a Dating folder, then the year we were married (2009), and so forth.

MAGIC BUT REAL

Love photos but overwhelmed by the idea of organizing them yourself no matter how you cut it? Hire a photo organizer. Yes, that's a thing. A very valuable thing if you ask me. If photos matter to you, they have to be organized—they just don't have to be organized by you. Delegate what you hate. Your family photos won't be any less valuable just because you didn't organize them. You'll have not only organized photos, but also: peace.

So why do photos "have" to be organized? Well, they don't. However, I like the idea of my kids being able to see the evolution of their childhood and even parts of their early adulthood when they get older because we kept an organized archive of photos. School photos, photos from work projects we've done together, or even photos they've taken with a Polaroid we gifted them are all kept in the family photo archive.

Here's what I don't want, for me or for you: that archiving family photos should become a daunting task. It should be a task that you know requires effort but to which you're willing to give that effort because the results are worth it. This doesn't have to be something you do five days in a row for twelve hours every day. (I would hope not.) What I've found is that scheduling ten to thirty minutes a week for organizing the family photo archive will quickly put a dent in the process.

Moving forward, I've scheduled two hours every first Sunday of the month to organize the family photo archive. Because I have designated a time and a day to do so, I can make sure nothing else is on my calendar at that time on that day. This is also a wonderful activity to tackle during thinking time, which we discussed in chapter 6.

As far as physical photos and school projects are concerned, I use a box (for each kid) with hanging folders. I label each folder with a grade. In the folder, I keep school photos, special photos, and any awards that child has won. I keep these boxes in our home office so they're easy to locate. The physical stuff matters too. My mom still has a laminated Mother's Day certificate I made for her—from 1990. The fact that she still has it makes her the MVP.

MAGIC MEMO

Laminate paper items that are most meaningful. It makes them last longer—and waterproof.

Your family photo archive is great for everyday photos you don't want to forget and want the kids to see as they grow up. I love everyday photos, but there is something special about intentionally arranging for family photos to be taken by a photographer. It's not the easiest thing to coordinate or schedule, but it is definitely worth it.

GROUP FAMILY PHOTOS

Have you ever scrolled your Facebook or Instagram timeline and seen people who have beautiful family photos and wondered, "How did they do that?" I know I did when I first started having kids. Getting a family to take a picture together, getting everyone to smile at the same time without wrinkling or staining their clothes—it seemed like a superpower that I just hadn't acquired yet. It seemed that the beautiful family photo happened in one take in the moment on the fly.

That's a lie.

As someone who takes photos for work every single week, that description is a lie even when you see me in a great photo at my house. It typically takes about one hundred to two hundred frames, one to two hours of planning, and some wonderful editing thanks to

Adobe Lightroom to get a usable shot. And I've been doing this for more than ten years.

I remember watching Kim Kardashian on a TV show once. During the interview, the host praised Kim's recent holiday family photo. Kim then candidly explained how her oldest did not want to take a photo that day and refused to get in the photo. They ended up taking her photo later and photoshopping her into the family photo to make it look like she was in the original!

Spoiler: taking family photos is hard because you have to capture everyone at the same time. And if your family is anything like mine, everyone is their own person with their own moods. It's really a gamble to get it done. Last year was the first time we took an official group family photo as a family of five. We did a session a couple of years ago for Halloween in our costumes and got some really good ones. All of my kids actually leaned in and gave us some great shots. It lasted about ten minutes and that was it. But hey, I'll take what I can get. Fewer things are more aesthetically pleasing than a family photo with everyone together. I believe it's worth it.

MAGIC BUT REAL

I always swear to the heavens above that I am going to make sure we take family photos every year. And every year, I fail miserably. Why? Because I don't plan ahead. I think I can pull it off in the last few days of November and that is way too late. Not only because photographers are usually all booked by then or getting ready to take off, but there's just not enough time. And I don't want to just "pull it off." I want it done well if I'm even going to bother doing it. By the time I pay a photographer, decide on a location, pick out and buy everyone's clothes, and then figure out my own hair and makeup, it better be good. Here's what I've learned the hard way: because taking care of all those decisions requires a lot of time, I need to book family photos *months* in advance. If I think it's too much time, it's likely just enough. Three months will pass by like a week!

Just this week I scheduled what will be our first professional Christmas photo session as a family of five. I am four months ahead of Christmas, and I've already made the necessary decisions. I don't want to fall into the trap of being unprepared. That's the worst feeling, and for family photos I want to feel my best.

I booked the photographer. She offered family mini shoots with a location already selected, so we will be shooting for only twenty-five minutes, which is perfect. The kids will barely last ten. I booked it early enough in the day when the kids won't be exhausted or in a bad mood. Our slot is at 9:00 a.m., which is great. The kids will have been awake for a couple of hours and it'll still be a few hours before naptime. I'll also have a call beforehand with the photographer to confirm what the vision is for our photos.

MAGIC MEMO

Even if booking a photographer is not in your budget, you can still make a family photo happen. Whether you have your own camera or your smartphone, have everyone in your family wear something nice and similar and prop your phone up on a tripod (or something like a tripod) and take advantage of your self-timer. When we do this, I always love how the photos turn out—they're not perfect, but they are MAGIC.

The goal is never perfection, it's connection. And photos are a way to connect to your memories.

I've also gone ahead and retrieved directions from our house to the location and added a thirty-minute cushion for parking and walking to where we need to be. Plus, kids. Children delay you in a way that is unmatched, and even if we are miraculously on time, it's better to be safe than sorry. So even though our shoot is at 9:00 a.m., our goal is to be there and ready at 8:30.

On the commute we'll listen to music or let the kids watch something that gets them in a chipper mood. Also, there will be no eating until afterward and only water to drink. I'll keep everyone's top layer neatly in the trunk to avoid any wrinkling or marks. I also have a battery-operated steamer that I'll be sure to bring with me as backup.

We do a big official family photo only once a year, so I pull out all the stops. Makeup artist, battery-operated steamer, booking months in advance. Whatever it takes within my means to get it done right.

If you're looking to get family photos done at a certain time, here's a timeline to help you schedule:

When to Book	When to Shoot	When to Receive Photos
July/August	September/October	Top of holiday season (November)
January/February	March/April	May
May/June	July/August	September

The goal should be to book three to four months out from when you want the actual photos in hand to use for holiday cards, framed for your home, or as gifts. Depending on the availability of your photographer and their process, you likely won't get photos until three to four weeks after shooting.

FAMILY YEARBOOK

So we've talked about organizing your photos, archiving your photos, and even getting professional family photos taken. Now, it's time to put all of those photos together in your family yearbook. I started doing a family yearbook in 2020 when we officially became a family of five, and I'm never going back. We surprised both my parents and my in-laws with a photo book of the kids and had a version made for ourselves. It was one of those things that make you wonder, "Why haven't I been doing this all along?"

Here's what I love about the family yearbook: you can include whomever you want. Photos of the kids, your pets, friends who have become family, coaches, neighbors, or members of your church. The goal of your family yearbook is to capture photos that tell the story of your family for that year.

Recently remarried and now you have a blended family?

Single mom with the best kid on the planet?

Had your first baby and couldn't wait to capture being a family of three?

Newly engaged or married and haven't had photos taken yet?

These are all fantastic reasons to create a family yearbook. When you're intentional about doing this every so often (some people do annual, but you can do it every other year), it's so special.

Every family is different, special, and worthy to be captured. It's easy to tell ourselves why we shouldn't get pictures done or promise ourselves we'll do it "when we lose weight" or say that "the kids won't even remember." But those are excuses. Don't delay creating family photo memories because your family isn't perfect. No family is. And years from now, you're going to wish you had photos of the time your toddler ate spaghetti for the first time and got it all over her face. Or the time you went to the pool with your neighbors who are still dear friends. Or even when you got your first family pet. Moments with your family matter even when they seem "small." Wonderful memories caught in a quick snapshot on your phone also belong in your family yearbook.

Again, this doesn't have to be an expensive effort—you can have photos printed at your local drugstore and create an old-school photo album. The family yearbook is an intentional way to capture your memories for reference later.

What's great about a family yearbook is that it is a normal thing that many photo companies offer as a service now. You can simply google "family yearbook," and you'll get a slew of options. (I received about seventy-one million results to be exact.) All you'll have to do is provide the photos (often digitally) and select your preferences like page layout and cover design. These sites provide so many options that it's almost impossible to not find what you like. Many of the options end up being under $100—a pretty reasonable price tag on commemorating your family memories for the last year.

CAPTURE TO REMEMBER

Even if you don't consider yourself a "picture person," I still encourage you to capture photos and videos consistently so you have the memories. And photos don't have to be professional to matter.

My oldest loves looking back at memories from previous birthdays, holidays, special moments, or even vacations we've taken together. She always starts off the conversation, "Mom, remember the time…" She even likes watching some of the vlogs on my YouTube channel that capture us on vacation or during a special moment.

In case you've been wondering how or where to group all of your family photos in a physical way, I encourage you to create a family yearbook. It's absolutely worth it.

If your family is art, then your family photo archive is the museum. And when you organize photos, plan an annual family photo, and create a family yearbook, you're making your memories MAGIC. You get the honor of curating, storing, and exhibiting the moments shared—be it everyday or special moments; digital or physical—for future reference whenever someone in your family goes, "Remember the time…"

CHAPTER NINE

MAGIC Moments Matter

Make a big deal and throw a party.

I was twenty-four when Chris and I got engaged. He comes from a big family like I do, so when it was time to visit his extended family in New Orleans, I was nervous. Meeting family can always be nerve-racking, and on top of that it was Thanksgiving. We were headed to his uncle's house, where everyone from aunts, uncles, and cousins to his grandmother would be gathered. On the day before Thanksgiving, we got to the door and we could hear music blasting. His uncle opened the door and embraced Chris and hugged me like we were already family. I walked into the kitchen to meet his entire family in a second line with napkins, umbrellas, and drinks in their hands. (A second line is a foot-led parade popular in New Orleans that's done in celebration.) I like to party, and so does my large West African family, but this still caught me off guard. When I walked in, GrandMaw-Maw grabbed me by the hand and said, "If you're going to be in this family, you got to know how to party." It was then that I understood celebrating is important because it can instantly make a stranger feel like family.

I've always enjoyed celebrating special occasions. Any excuse to have a party is my default, and it's my parents' fault. They always threw parties—for their anniversary, my and my sister's birthdays, and even the holidays—when I was growing up, and they always made people feel welcome. When I was four they threw me a My Little Pony birthday party with an ice cream cake that made me feel like the coolest kid in the world. When my sister turned sixteen, they threw her a SpongeBob SquarePants (her favorite show as a kid) party where her cake was the entire Bikini Bottom. We were far from rich, so these parties weren't overly elaborate like you may have seen on an episode of *My Super Sweet 16*. However, my parents were thoughtful, considerate, and made you feel like a part of the family whether you were a first cousin or a next-door neighbor.

If you like to celebrate, then celebrate. Don't let anyone make you feel silly for wanting to have a party or to get together because it's your birthday, you got a new job, or it's your favorite holiday. There are many horrible things going on in the world, so finding a reason to celebrate the good stuff is a godsend. As someone who always gets excited to host a MAGIC celebration, I can tell you that it's always better when you plan.

MAGIC MEMO

A MAGIC celebration is a special occasion in your or a family's life—birthday, anniversary, holiday, baby or bridal shower, for example—that you deem worth celebrating in a meaningful, aesthetically pleasing, goal-oriented, intentional, and consistent way.

INVITES

Celebrations matter because they're a chance to have special moments with the people in your life. A celebration is a way of saying, "This moment is meaningful, and you matter to me, so let's fellowship together over food and drink." Simply inviting someone is meaningful because it's your way of showing that you thought of them and wanted them to be included in your celebration. I'm old-school and love to send personalized invitations. Whether they're digital or physical, it's always important to use someone's name. If you're inviting one of your kids' classmates to their party, go the extra mile and touch base with the teacher to get a list of everyone in the class and spell everyone's name right. Spelling people's names correctly is a big deal. Think about how you feel when someone spells or says your name wrong. It never feels right. Taking the extra step to do this makes people feel special and like you invited them to the occasion with forethought.

Digital invitations are totally expected nowadays and can be sent via text or email. If you're going to text invitations, text everyone personally, even the people you know really well. It's easier to keep a digital paper trail this way and then you can easily copy and paste the invite before personalizing the message. I know group text messaging is a thing, but I highly recommend individually texting each person their invite so that you (1) avoid giving people's numbers to other people they don't know; and (2) can make sure your message goes through to everyone based on what kind of phone they have.

Even when an invite is digital, I encourage you to personalize it with the person's or family's name. We all know what it feels like to be group messaged and spam messaged—you never respond to the message with a sense of urgency or you simply just ignore it. When you want guests to respond to you and RSVP, use their name and spell it correctly. For good measure, I even like creating prewritten replies to guests based on their responses. In your Notes app, write out something along the lines of "Looking forward to seeing you" or "You'll be missed—thanks for letting me know" to quickly respond to general RSVPs. (If something more layered than "No, we can't make it" is the reply, respond accordingly.)

For email, there are quite a few options you can use to invite guests via their in-box. Of course, you want to prep by getting all your guests' email addresses (spelled correctly!) before sending out invitations. Usually just sending guests a text to their main email address is the way to go because you can simply copy and paste it.

MAGIC BUT REAL

If you're not a great host or you simply don't like to be around a lot of people all at once, you don't have to celebrate with a party at all. You might be someone who prefers more intimate settings like a lunch or dinner with close friends and that's totally fine. Simply make a reservation and invite friends to come enjoy the occasion with you. The restaurant or venue can do the heavy lifting of logistics depending on how much you want to do at the restaurant. Not the best at planning but still like parties and celebrating? Hire it out. Party planners exist for a reason—to plan parties better than you do, so you can sit back and enjoy.

ACCOMMODATIONS

What makes an occasion meaningful to others is the way you accommodate them. I feel like the best accommodations are often made ahead of time because you thought of someone and their needs before they even occurred. Sure, you're not a mind reader and shouldn't be expected to be one. Making accommodations isn't about perfectly predicting the future; rather, it's about thoughtfully planning according to people's specific needs. If you're asking someone to have dinner with you for your birthday or any other special occasion—whether at a restaurant or in your home—consider their dietary needs. If you have a vegan friend, will there be vegan options? Is there someone in the group who recently gave up alcohol? Maybe you can include sparkling cider as an option for your toast. Diabetic relatives? Is there a sugar-free option to include in the treats? Do they have special needs? Maybe they have to bring their kid?

My entire reason for writing this book is because I want women to understand that there's joy in not being everything and still being more than enough. When you accommodate your guests at your MAGIC occasions, you're saying, "You may be different, but you're more than enough, and I'm happy to accommodate that." If you're unable to accommodate, there's nothing wrong with that because again, you can't (and shouldn't) be everything to everyone. Be honest and direct when asked if you can accommodate certain needs. If you believe that your best efforts to accommodate won't be sufficient for their needs, then hold out on inviting them.

One of my favorite things about the MAGIC of occasions is how they look. A MAGIC occasion should be aesthetically pleasing because it matters. Balloon garlands, Christmas trees, and decorated pumpkins can be an instant mood booster and get everyone attending excited for the celebration. Being excited is part of the celebration as well. It certainly doesn't have to be Pinterest-perfect, but making an occasion aesthetically pleasing absolutely makes the occasion more memorable. This doesn't mean you have to go overboard or spend a lot of money. It's always about planning ahead and thinking about the experience.

The foolproof, cheaper go-to decor for special occasions is almost always balloons. Get a fifty or one hundred pack and a $20 electric air pump and go to town. If helium is more your speed, you can buy a helium tank or order a few dozen helium balloons. Balloons instantly make a room feel like a party and work for every budget. They're also ideal if you're throwing something together at the last minute.

MAGIC MOMENT

As I was in the midst of finishing up this book, my dad's birthday, my wedding anniversary (the same day!), and my oldest child's birthday all fell within the same week.

We threw a last-minute birthday party for our oldest, and if writing books and this whole influencer thing doesn't work out, Hubs and I should throw kids' birthday parties for a living. We have lots of nieces and nephews, and it's always nice to see our loved ones—kids and adults— together having a good time. We threw a unicorn party, with a bouncy house (always a hit with kids) and a little picnic seating area with a low table. We got unicorn- themed paper plates and party hats and a dozen throw pillows along with a picnic blanket from Target. Hubs went overboard on the balloons—he ordered six dozen— which really did the heavy lifting for us. Especially if you're throwing together a last-minute MAGIC celebration and want it to look good—balloons are the way to go. If possible, though, still plan a full day ahead of time to give yourself peace. Maizah's birthday party turned out beautifully without any stress.

Pinterest is always my go-to for inspiration whenever I'm having a MAGIC occasion for my kids or the holidays. I have secret boards for each of the kids' birthdays. Whenever I notice they're into a certain show or character throughout the year, I'll pin a few themed ideas to their board. I mentioned in the "Time Is MAGIC" chapter that I have talking time with the kids at bedtime—this is where we discuss what they want to do for their birthdays. We discuss this all year long because, guess what? Kids never tire of talking about their birthdays. (Neither do I; birthdays are fun to talk about.)

If you're crafty and up for DIY projects, there are many great ideas on Pinterest. Go crazy. And even if you're not crafty, Pinterest is a great place for gathering ideas for whatever MAGIC occasions you have coming up in your life. This is also where I find fantastic Etsy vendors who make the cutest party favors, custom wrapping paper, and more unique ideas. Whether you're planning it or having someone else do it, having photos that you can reference all in one place is always nice. Secret Pinterest boards for your MAGIC occasion celebration are a huge help.

RUN OF SHOW

The day of any MAGIC celebration—whether it's a surprise party or Thanksgiving dinner—can get hectic with all the moving parts. The goal is to have things run as smoothly as possible so everyone can enjoy the MAGIC. You as well. So even if you're hosting, don't be afraid to ask for help, have decorations or food delivered, or even hire it out to make things run smoothly. Always, always, always create a run of show for a MAGIC celebration—ahead of time—to be aware of all the moving parts.

I love having parties. I am not the best at planning them, however. I want to host, then I want to enjoy, then I want to host again, but then I get hungry and I want to eat. You have to be honest with yourself about who you are, and understand you're not everything. And even though everything must get done for the celebration, it doesn't all have to be done by you. Understanding that and making decisions accordingly will free you and make the celebration much more enjoyable.

What's not enjoyable is planning a party in real time as it's happening. You don't have to be the only one making decisions. If we're having a celebration at my house, Hubs and I tag team together, even if it's only in decision making, to be like, "Hey, here's what's going on." I'm good at people; Hubs is good at logistics. For a long time, I thought that it was my duty to become better at logistics. It's not. Not even a little bit. It is my job to know that I'm not good at logistics and to ask for help in that area. If it's not at our home, I will hire out logistics to spare myself being overwhelmed and experiencing temporary failure.

The run of show doesn't have to be elaborate—in fact, the simpler the better. Grab a piece of paper and write down what you want to happen the day of the celebration and in what order. Edit it until it's what you want and then stick to the plan. Sure, little things may happen, and you might be off by ten to fifteen minutes, and that's fine. The goal is to know what's happening and approximately when.

This doesn't apply just to parties (like birthdays, anniversaries, and showers) but also to holidays. I take Christmas pretty seriously and always want Christmas morning to be special. I thought that would happen simply because I wished. But guess what, that is not what happens. After the kids open their gifts, the living room is a mess, and everyone's famished, ready to eat breakfast. Last year, I created a brief yet clear run of show where we opened gifts and then I assigned the kids, their aunt, and their grandparents to tidy the living room while Chris and I made breakfast. We didn't have to guess what was next because it was already decided. That makes those MAGIC occasions even more special because you're aware of how your time is going to be used. Breakfast doesn't have to be at eight on the dot, but once the gifts are opened no one should have to ask, "What are we doing for breakfast?" Creating a run of show for your celebrations turns your good intentions into great action items.

FOOD, PERSONALIZATIONS, AND THANK-YOUS

One of the best parts about a celebration is that you have to eat, and people will always show up for free food. When you're entertaining more than six people, unless you're a cook, chef, or baker, this is an opportune time to order catering or delivery. Not only is there no shame in that, there's honor in it. Cooking for a lot of people is a lot of work, and, honestly, your time can be better spent if that's not your forte. Aside from special treats like a pound cake (my family swears by mine) or a nice cheese or snack board, order pizza or your preferred takeout and call it a day. In almost a decade of throwing birthday parties for my kids, I've never once had anyone complain about having pizza. Never!

MAGIC MEMO

Whatever you think is the right amount of food, order 25 percent extra. Anytime I have ordered what I believed was the exact amount of needed food, I always came up short. If someone asked for seconds, they were out of luck. Sure, they were more than fine with that, but when someone shows up to my house or party to eat, I want to make sure I can feed them to their satisfaction. If you think six pizzas is enough, order the seventh. If you think the medium bucket of chicken will suffice, just grab the large. If there's extra, people are always happy to take leftovers, and both my mom and my mother-in-law say, "It's better to have more than less" when it comes to food. The two moms are right!

Let me tell you what makes kids and adults feel special: when something is personalized for them. This can be a number of things: name cards, goody bags, and party souvenirs with their names are always a hit. Think about how you feel when you see your name on something—it makes you feel like a star! Anytime I can do this, I include personalization in the celebration to elevate aesthetics and to make the attendees feel really special. We went to a birthday party for our good friend Ashley's son, and in the goody bags she gave each kid a water bottle with their name on it. It was especially a hit because it was the beginning of summer. Her intentionality blew us away. Even a name tag on a goody bag goes a long way.

One thing worth being intentional about is saying thank you to guests for coming to the occasion you put together—no matter how big or small. Saying "Thank you" is a small gesture that makes a big deal in the long run. People didn't have to take time out of their day to spend it with me and my loved ones, so I don't take it lightly. Besides how much I love pretty decorations and good food, the people are what makes a celebration so fantastic. The thank-you doesn't have to be formal or over-the-top. Simply sending out sincere and heartfelt thank-you texts works just fine. A handwritten note will never go out of style, though, and shows that you really care and thought about who you're writing to. (I always feel deeply considered when someone sends me a handwritten card.) If your budget permits, sending out thank-you cards within a month or so of your celebration—especially if gifts were received—is always appreciated. Etiquette experts advise that you must say thank you within a superspecific time frame, but I don't think it's ever too late to say thank you. However, setting a goal, with a reminder in place, of doing so within a month after the celebration will not allow too much time to pass and will help you not to forget. There are many stationery and card companies out there that allow you to order thank-you cards and personalize them online. After my daughter's seventh birthday party, we sent a cute thank-you card with her picture on it a couple of days later, specifically thanking each person for the gift they gave. Most times, people expect that sort of thing after a wedding or a baby shower. However, I'm all about doing the most to raise the bar and exude excellence for almost all things in my life. Saying thank you is one of those things. Even after a kid's birthday party.

TRADITIONS

I take all celebrations pretty seriously, but Christmastime is when I really commit. I've been hosting Christmas at my house for the last few years and I feel fortunate to be able to do so. I remember how wonderful it was growing up and how special my parents made Christmas. I want to be able to do the same for my kids and my family as well. Creating traditions that take special celebrations from good to great doesn't have to be deep, just deliberate and consistent.

Matching family pajamas started as a lucky coincidence when I was in Target a few years ago and I was able to find everyone's sizes all at the same time. (That never happens.) But everyone was so excited that we all matched when we woke up Christmas morning that I knew it was worth the effort of repeating. Matching Christmas pajamas is now a family tradition that we all look forward to.

MAGIC MEMO

Nothing about a tradition should feel forced for the sake of social media or acting like something you're not. If your family isn't the type to watch Hallmark movies in December, no need to fake it. Traditions are a way to create a consistent MAGIC occasion with your family. It's about realizing how something you enjoyed can be repeated, but if it can't—don't try.

What traditions mean the most to you and your family?

What do you and your family most enjoy doing together?

How can you create new traditions that matter and add to your family MAGIC?

The very first Christmas we hosted at our home, we had game night on Christmas Eve and laughed until our sides hurt. It was one of those things that surprisingly ended up bringing all of us much joy, so now we repeat it with little touches of MAGIC—matching mugs with hot chocolate—while playing Christmas music in the background.

Now, I intentionally shop for matching family Christmas pajamas in September (I always have them purchased by the end of September); and I buy everyone in my family (Hubs, the kids, my mom and dad, who spend the holiday with us) monogrammed mugs for hot chocolate. On Christmas Eve, when we're all together, I present them to everyone before bath time, so everyone has their mug and pajamas before we get into game night. Then we play the same games we always do every Christmas Eve because if it ain't broke, don't fix it. Again, traditions and the MAGIC they hold don't have to be fancy; they just have to matter to you and those you share them with.

MAGIC MEMO

Traditions are MAGIC because they become consistent celebrations that everyone looks forward to being a part of.

Celebrations don't take place every day, but when they happen they should be MAGIC. That requires a level of intentionality and deliberate planning ahead of time that should be taken seriously. Whether it's PawPaw retiring or Christmas Eve game night, make traditions that matter to you, decorate in a fun and festive way that gets everyone excited, and say thank you to those who helped make the celebration memorable with their attendance.

CHAPTER TEN

The MAGIC of Balance, Boundaries, and Having a Village

When you lack boundaries, you lack balance.
When you a lack village, you lack belonging.

One of the most common questions I get from everyday women is "How do you find balance?" And for a while there, I was truly convinced that balance was a unicorn and didn't actually exist. But the truth is, balance looks different for everyone based on the season they're in and their goals in life.

Balance doesn't mean giving equal parts of yourself to everything in your life. It means giving higher quality of yourself to the things you currently value most (priorities). It's impossible to equally divide yourself up to handle everything in your life without stretching yourself too thin.

I have always been the kind of person to have a full plate. Doing a lot makes me feel valuable, useful, and important in a situation. In my senior year of high school, I was the sports editor for my school newspaper, in the court at the winter formal, and a cheerleader. My journalism teacher would spring last-minute stories on me, my cheerleading coach would schedule last-minute practices, and if anyone needed someone to help with a project, I'd volunteer.

As I related earlier, when I left college and moved to NYC, I worked Monday through Friday as a temporary assistant at the corporate offices of Macy's while also moonlighting as an assistant for my friend who was a club promoter. Both of my bosses could call me anytime and I would jump to make sure they had what they needed. In most cases, I would give them more than they asked for. This way of life often left me scatterbrained and stressed out, while I would watch friends who had just as much on their plate—sometimes more—seem calm, cool, and collected.

When I became a wife and mom, the pattern continued. I wanted to do all the things—be a good wife, a wonderful mother, work a nine-to-five job trying to be my boss's favorite, and grow my blog to be successful and profitable. I'd also never miss any of my friends' birthdays or special occasions, and I'd say yes to my extended family whenever they needed me.

And guess what would happen? In many of those situations, I would fall short. I would be late, forget to bring what I'd committed to contributing, and end up miserable and exhausted. Balance was nonexistent because I had no boundaries in place.

Balance allows making time and space for the priorities in your life while boundaries create the limits for those priorities.

It wasn't until I had Caliana—my second child—that I started to set boundaries. For me, going from one to two kids was intense. But it was the first time I started saying no and feeling at peace with the decision I'd made. I started to be explicitly honest with myself about my bandwidth and limits. Showing up 100 percent for whatever I committed to mattered, so I understood that would require setting up parameters that I'd lacked in the past. It also required me to unlearn lies I'd told myself for so long.

The truth about balance is that it is a standard. A boundary is an understanding. The only way you can position yourself and others to meet your standards is with understanding. But until you get clear on what that understanding is, you will not be able to articulate it, let alone enforce it.

Think of your everyday life as a multilane highway where each lane represents a priority in your life. The lines on the road indicate boundaries (designated space for your priorities). You're free to switch lanes as often as you'd like. Depending on the day, you might be in the far left lane moving fast the majority of the day because you have to get something done quickly for that priority (like a deadline for work). On another day, you might stay in a far right lane because you need to take your time and that priority requires a slower pace (like a screen fast with your family).

You're not supposed to drive in two lanes at the same time because it's risky and creates confusion while driving—aka a lack of balance while living your everyday life. For instance, you can't take your kids to work with you and your spouse shouldn't be with you on a self-care day. Driving on the shoulder of the highway (distractions) indicates that you're veering from your priorities and need to get back in a lane to continue driving—aka living—safely. Driving on the shoulder is possible, but it often creates wear and tear on your vehicle—aka you—which forces you to come to an unplanned and unexpected stop to recover.

The beauty of this is that you get to choose what type of vehicle you're going to be, your priority lanes, and where and how you're going to drive within your boundaries. But not everyone is going your speed or direction, which is why boundaries are so necessary.

Setting boundaries requires courage because you often have to fight internal wars to convince yourself to set them. You lie to yourself, saying, "You're being unreasonable," "You can do it," or "Just this one time." You deserve to tell yourself the truth so you can make decisions within your boundaries. Boundaries are created to protect yourself based on the priorities in your life. It's your personal responsibility to protect what you prioritize because when you lack protection, it's hard to prosper.

I'm here to tell you, no matter how scary it is, your personal boundary **WARS** are worth fighting. Here are the four everyday boundaries (WARS) you should set to find more balance and every-day MAGIC in your life:

Work/life boundary

Access boundary

Relationship boundary

Space boundary

WORK/LIFE BOUNDARY

It is possible to love both your life and your work. Your family is a priority and so is your career or business. However, family comes first. That doesn't make you any less of a career woman or businesswoman, or mother, for that matter. It just is what it is and the boundaries you create for your life and work reflect that. When you're at home with your family, be all in. Be all hands on deck and committed to doing your thing as a wife and/or a mom. Don't dilute the quality of your time with family by trying to multitask by answering emails while you're having movie night with the kids. Zero in and be present with your family intentionally, willingly, and guilt-free. That way when it's time to go to work, you have created the space to be all in there without the guilt as well. We spend more waking hours at work (just like the kids do at school) than with our families during the week. That's just the reality of it. Even so, when it's time to work, even if you work from home, your boundary has to be respected. It's a healthy thing for families—especially the kids—to understand. My kids know that Mommy works on her business downstairs in her office. When I'm working, they know not to interrupt unless necessary. Usually they're at school, but when they're on a break and I still have to work, the boundaries are understood and respected. Encourage your family to respect yours as well. And when it's time for dinner or family time, work stuff can kick rocks. Tackle it the next time work is scheduled.

What work/life boundaries do you need to put in place to create more everyday MAGIC?

What do boundaries in your life look like to you? What do boundaries at work look like?

MAGIC MOMENT

When you email me or anyone from my team, there's an autoresponse that goes out telling you when we'll get back to you if it's after hours because family is one of our company values and everyone on my team is a parent. Hopefully, we're in the aftermath of the "hustle, hustle, hustle, work, work, work" spin on all things professional, but it has always been important to me that I do my thing at work, but that I do my thing at home as well, and there are certain times for each of those things. If we work together, that boundary must be respected.

ACCESS BOUNDARY

The boundary that tends to get crossed in a lot of cases is the access boundary. Rules regarding who has access to you and when they have access to you are a very big deal and shouldn't be created without deliberate thought. Here's what you have to know from the get-go: only you get to decide that. There is no person on this planet who should have access to you 24/7. Not one. Only my Lord and Savior has unlimited access to me at all times. That's it. My spouse and kids have the most access to me, but when I need a break, whether I need to pee or need a weekend to myself, I will make the necessary arrangements to do so whenever I see fit. If someone calls and you don't want to talk, you can give them a call back when you're ready. If you don't want to accept an invitation because you'd rather rest, then rest it is. Your life—your marriage, your motherhood, your friendships, your work, your social life—should not feel like a prison just because you prioritize too many things. Anytime you feel shackled to an aspect of your life, figure out how to free yourself figuratively or physically and create the necessary access boundaries. Sometimes that requires explicit honesty and having hard conversations with others, but so be it. Anything else results in resentment, feeling overwhelmed, and burnout, which just isn't worth it. This isn't synonymous with avoiding responsibilities or overlooking commitments. If you committed beforehand and told someone you would do something, then do it. But in the end if you realize it was a bit much for you to show up in that way, be honest with yourself and tweak your availability to such commitments in the future. Maybe you can in fact show up to dinner and drinks with friends, but weeknights work better for you because you don't want to give up the uninterrupted quality time you have with your family on the weekends. Radical self-honesty spares you from the burden of guilt and gives you the boost you need to create the necessary access boundaries in your life.

Have access boundaries been an issue for you recently?

What can you do to ensure your access boundaries are honored day to day?

RELATIONSHIP BOUNDARY

We have so many relationships in our lives that we underestimate most of them. They affect us in huge ways, so having specific boundaries within each one determines their quality. A relationship boundary allows you to define what you're comfortable with and how you would like to be treated by whomever you're in a relationship with. While we usually assume that we mean romantic relationships when we talk about relationship boundaries, the truth is boundaries apply to any of your relationships, especially the ones you value most. The relationships you have with your partner, your children, your siblings, your parents, and your closest friends require healthy boundaries to flourish. Have the conversations necessary to establish boundaries and explain how you would like your relationship to go. In some cases, you'll have to have this conversation more than once, but it's important so your relationships aren't strained due to violated boundaries.

One question you can ask those you have close relationships with is: "How can I be a better [_____] to you?" Chris and I tend to ask each other this question every year on our anniversary, but it's also something I ask the kids and my close friends. It's a way to create openness, expectations, and boundaries at a very honest level.

SPACE BOUNDARY

Last but not least are the boundaries of your space. Your space isn't solely limited to your home—this can apply to your workspace, bedroom, bathroom, or even your car. But it's important to put boundaries in place for your space, especially if you're in a season of your life where you have to share your space with others regularly. Sure, your mom taught you to share growing up, but being assertive about the boundaries surrounding your space is important to maintain peace of mind and, sometimes, privacy. The kids have reign in most spaces in our house, but for the most part our bedroom is a no-kid zone. It's the one room that gets to be a sanctuary for myself and my husband, and I'm happy to use my serious mom voice to reestablish that boundary if need be. If you really like your car and don't want food in it, enforce that boundary. Work from home and don't have your own office but you have a desk that you like to be organized and untouched? Enforce that boundary. Obsessed with your sneakers and don't want anyone in your family messing around in your closet? Enforce that boundary.

The people who love you most can't respect a boundary that you don't enforce. People who know and love you most don't have a crystal ball. Be open to sharing what your boundaries are—especially when they're new—so they can be honored. There is absolutely nothing wrong with having boundaries. If you don't have boundaries, it will be impossible to maintain the everyday MAGIC in your life.

We've established balance and boundaries; now let's discuss the people who help us win our WARS: our villages.

IT TAKES A VILLAGE TO MAKE MAGIC

Eleven years ago, our car was repossessed and our electricity was turned off.

I tried blogging full-time for two years with not one clue what I was doing. We had been married for two years, and we thought if Chris quit his job and we put all our energy into creating content together, the money would come.

That is not what happened, friends.

We fought, like, every day because of the stress of having no money and no clue what we were doing.

Our dear friends Tony and Ashley took us in while we got our sh-t together. I will forever be grateful to them for doing so.

After weeks of applying for jobs online, I got a full-time job, Chris got a new job, and we secretly dreamed of working together again, but fear never let us peacefully discuss the idea in depth.

A couple of years ago, we had a breakthrough in couples' therapy about what was holding us back. It was the breakthrough that led Chris to leave his corporate gig of nine years (the job he got after our clueless season) and come on full-time as the COO of our company.

The circumstances are radically different because: alignment.

Early on, not only were we not in alignment with God's plan for us, but we were not in alignment with each other. (At all.)

I learned (the long and hard way) that you can't reap in the same season you sow. But even when you make the mistake of thinking you can, His faithfulness will always be greater than your faults. But this time His faithfulness was not only in alignment between me and Chris, but also with our friendship with Tony and Ashley.

Their selflessness and willingness to open up their home to us for two months while we were getting ourselves on our feet is something that I will never forget. It makes me tear up as I write about it. They never judged. They never snuck in smart remarks. They listened to us as we vented to them through the process. They kept speaking to us afterward. LOL. Jokes aside, I am deeply grateful to them for doing that for us. It was such a remarkable lesson on friendship and God's goodness.

I know God is real; just look at my friends.

We are insanely fortunate to have the friends and family that we have. They are the most meaningful people in our lives. They always show up for us and that is something I am wildly grateful for. I am the oldest of two and Hubs is the second-oldest of four. (With the exception of one, we all live in the same city.) We're close with our parents, who live within ten miles of our house, and they all get along with one another. Our best friends are just that—the *best*. They're the kind of people you ask to be the godparents of your kids and that's exactly what we did. If we count our own, all of our siblings' kids, and our best friends' kids, there are seventeen kids total. That, my friends, is a village for you. They say it takes a village to raise a child. That's also what it takes to build a life of MAGIC.

I understand that this is not everyone's reality. Relationships and friendships are delicate and will not look the same for everyone. Whether your village is big or small, full of blood relatives or wonderful friends from stages of your life, it doesn't make it any less valuable. Maybe you are close with your siblings and parents, but you live in a different state than they do. Your village can include one of your kid's teachers or principal, a neighbor, church members, or old college roommates who have become like family. Extended family can also serve as your village. The point is to recognize those who have continuously shown up for you and tried to be of service as well.

All of us are valuable village people for different reasons. Find your reason—you'll often discover it by being honest with yourself—and commit to that. The beautiful thing about your village is that they're there for you at the times that matter.

EVERYDAY VILLAGE

I've mentioned it throughout this book, but we're so fortunate to have my mom watch Christian (our two-year-old) during the day while the girls are in school and Chris and I work. It's such a wonderful thing to have her watch her grandson throughout the week and they get to build a special bond. We also have the blessing of seeing my dad, my sister, and my in-laws on what I would consider nearly an everyday basis, meaning we usually see them at least once a week. Your village is made up of the people who matter most in your life, so creating space for you and your family to see them is important. My dad works from home throughout the week, so he likes to kick his weekend off by taking the kids to the park and buying them Happy Meals for dinner. They've deemed it "Grandpa Friday," and it's what the kids look forward to on Friday evenings after school. My father-in-law cuts our grass every other week, and the kids are always excited to see their PawPaw doing yard work. Even when they know they should be getting ready for bath time, they plead with me to go outside and "help" him, and it always works. Sometimes my mother-in-law will come on those days, too, and it becomes an instant "Grandma and PawPaw are here!" party. And when all four of the grandparents are around, we'll make it a day. The kids are on 10 until they leave. Our kids are so blessed to have grandparents who are alive and well and live nearby. I never want to dampen their spirits because of the schedule. I want them to relish spending time with their grandparents.

This is also what happens when my sister, Maya, comes over. The kids are always so excited when their Aunty Maya comes over, and they scream her name with glee when she walks through the door. Their relationship with her is so special. But honestly, all of the relationships we have within our village are special. The kids all love their cousins very much. My sisters-in-law inspire me and make me laugh to the point of tears. I'm very, very blessed to have such a village. It's something I do not take for granted. They have been there for us during such critical times in our lives and we do our best to show up for them in theirs.

What does your village look like?

If you don't have one, who are some people you would like to include in your village?

Who are some people from your family whom you can rely on? Friends? What about from work, school, and church?

TIMES THAT MATTER

We are not designed to do life alone, and that is the beauty of having a village. Trying to go through critical times in your life without encouragement, support, or help from those who love you is hard. It's worth listening to your village and making sure you've heard them, even if you don't agree. The goal isn't always agreement, but instead understanding. When you're understood, you feel validated, safe, and seen, which is an incredibly important gift from those we know, love, and trust.

Hard Times

When Chris and I separated a few years ago it was a really hard time for us. In addition to being emotionally spent, we were navigating the separation with work, parenting, therapy sessions, and deciding what we wanted for the future of our marriage. Outside of our immediate families, not many people knew what we were going through. I was afraid of the judgment of others and I didn't want to disappoint our village. But the village isn't there for you to impress. They're not your audience. They're your people, and they're there to help. But it's impossible for anyone to help you if you don't tell them what's wrong. Sure, they can assume and read the context clues—but when you say, "Hey, I'm not all right. This is what's going on with me," then they can show up directly and specifically for the current hell you're going through.

Our best friends Torrence and Erica—who are also a married couple—were really in our corner during that season. In fact, they were our accountability partners and were so patient and encouraging. They were able to do that without passing harsh judgment, crossing boundaries, or even being invasive, which still fascinates me. At the same time, they very much held us accountable. When we made the decision to stay married and work on our relationship, they were there to cheer us on while reminding us it wasn't going to be easy. They met us in person, even spent one very awkward Thanksgiving with us, and texted us consistently to encourage and keep us on track toward this new chapter in our marriage. It was hands down the hardest season in my adult life, and I don't know if I would've made it without their friendship. I learned that friendship is a gift that requires presence, patience, and persistence, just like any other important life relationship.

A few years later, Erica lost her grandmother, which was very hard for her and her family. She comes from a close-knit family, and losing their matriarch was just as devastating as you'd assume. Erica was working for me at the time as my photographer, and from the looks of it, my friend really needed time to grieve. She was heartbroken while still trying to be strong for her mom and navigate the daily tasks of being a wife and mom. One day when she came in for a shoot, she just broke down. I sat with her and listened to her share her favorite moments with her grandmother and let her grieve without interruption. Then I sent her home and told her not to worry about working for the next couple of months. I made sure she was paid during her time off and I figured it out. She would've done the same for me.

Being a good friend during hard times can literally save someone's life. I know it's easy to say, "It couldn't be me," and you're right. It couldn't. Because not everybody is for everyone. And not everyone should have access to your everyday life. But for the people who are in your village and in your corner, show up for them like their life depends on it. In some cases, it just might.

What do you need from your village during hard times?

How can you ask for help during a hard time so you don't have to go through it alone?

Busy Times

What's awesome about our village is that we all know what it's like to have small children and so it's easy to extend one another grace when our schedules make us busy. If you have a friend or relative in your village who offers to help you during a busy season, take them up on the offer. And even if they don't offer and you need help, ask. We are the kind of parents who run a tight ship at home and make sure that we don't miss too much of a beat when it comes to our daily schedules. Even when we're on a trip. But when we had to travel cross-country without our kids and both sets of grandparents were unavailable—the village came to the rescue.

They got to stay at Uncle Tony and Aunty Ashley's house while we flew to California for a wedding. We had seriously considered canceling our trip because we didn't want to impose our two kids (at the time) on anyone. But guess what? We hesitantly asked them if they'd be able to watch them and they gladly obliged. The kids had the best time ever and asked us when we were going on another trip so they could stay at Uncle Tony and Aunty Ashley's again. Ha!

Good Times

Every Memorial Day weekend we celebrate my birthday (which ends up falling on that weekend or a few days after) with a get-together to officially kick off the summer. It's become an unofficial annual touch base for our village as the kids are out of school and most people's availability is open. Especially over these last couple of years with all of our busy schedules coupled with social distancing restrictions—it ends up being the one time a year everyone in our village can get together at the same time and it's always a blast. We take a picture of all the kids to see how much everyone has grown and it's so cute to see the new additions join the bunch. We've been doing it for years and it fills me with great joy. These are the people we've grown up with as kids, and friends who were in our wedding, and now our kids get to grow up together. I love my village deeply and I pray overflow of blessings upon each of their households.

MAGIC MEMO

Make time to see your village outside of special moments at least once a year. Even when it's not a birthday or a

---

holiday, touch base with your village to see if you can get together on an upcoming weekend to simply spend time together. I get it—it's hard because we're all so busy. But you never know when people could use some face-to-face time for a laugh with loved ones and a break from life's stresses. You might not know it, but you could likely use it too.

Having a village isn't about having a bunch of yes-people around. It's about having a group of friends and family whom you can rely on, trust, encourage, support, celebrate, hold accountable, and be held accountable by. You show up for one another during the good times as well as the hard times, always with the common goal of rooting for one another to do well and win in life. When kids see this—adults as well—they're encouraged to be there for others, which is a valuable trait to have.

Don't just rely on your village, be reliable. Don't just ask your village to show up, show up for them as well. Building a strong village isn't about tit for tat but it is about the reciprocity of willingly being there for one another. Sure, it takes a village to raise a child. It also takes one to build a life full of MAGIC.

Everyday MAGIC is incredible, but impossible to achieve when you don't have boundaries that protect you and create balance or a village to share that everyday MAGIC with.

OUTRO

Why do they want to see all of these drafts before I post content? I just don't know how they expect me to do all of this work so soon," I cried.

"Well, isn't this what you want to do? You agreed to it, didn't you?" Hubs asked matter-of-factly.

"Yeah, but…"

"Well, babe. This is part of the work. You gotta practice how you play."

The truth was I had a demanding brand partner who was micromanaging every single piece of content I was creating for a brand campaign. As an influencer, I get paid a rate to create content and post it on Instagram, YouTube, or my blog while featuring or including a brand's product. It's something I've had the luxury of doing for the last seven years full-time and I absolutely love it. However, in this instance, the brand was super anal about all the details, asking for an abundance of edits to a video. If you've ever filmed and edited a video, you know how much work that is. That kind of work on a deadline coupled with motherhood is a lot.

The truth was, I had waited until the last minute to pull something off only for life to throw me a curveball in the form of a one-year-old in the process of sleep training and a four-year-old with a cold.

I was over it. I wanted to make an excuse and for that excuse to mean I could tell them I couldn't do it until it was more convenient for me. When things weren't naturally effortless for me, I would look for someone or something to blame so that the problem wasn't me. The truth was, I was the problem. How I handled my work wasn't thoughtful or responsible and when people started asking for results, I couldn't deliver. Nothing feels worse than promising you'll do something and not being able to deliver. I gave them my word and now, my actions and words weren't matching up. That's an integrity issue. I was willing to dilute my integrity for the sake of my comfort and lack of commitment, which is never good. I was overwhelmed and focused on the weight of the problem more than I thought about discovering a solution.

This is how a lot of early conversations in my career as an influencer would go. I would try to complain about the workload of being an influencer with my husband. As you can see, he's not one to throw me a pity party and would gladly put it all in perspective. Sure, he's always there for me when I need him, but he's right—you gotta practice how you play.

Everyday MAGIC is practice. MAGIC takes practice. Big

moments like vacations, birthdays, getting a new job, a new house, holidays, or any big, hard moments in your life are when you play. This is why everyday MAGIC is vital. It positions you to play for the not-so-everyday moments without fail. And let's be clear, practice doesn't make perfect. Practice makes permanent. The goal with everyday MAGIC isn't to make your life perfect; it's to live your life in meaningful, aesthetically pleasing, goal-oriented, intentional, and consistent ways that help you realize you're more than enough. MAGIC is a permanent practice in your life.

In her 2019 Netflix documentary *Homecoming*, Beyoncé said, "Most people don't want to practice because you look stupid when you practice." No one likes looking or feeling stupid. But trying doesn't make you stupid, even if you fall short; it simply means you're putting in the effort to do the work. Also, where the hell did we get the idea that we should be good at something simply because we did it once? You are not entitled to being good at things because you don't practice.

MAGIC MOMENT

"Well, that didn't work," I said matter-of-factly while laughing with my oldest as we looked at my banana chocolate chip cake Pinterest fail. A month prior to this moment, I had made some really delicious chocolate chip banana muffins and decided a cake version would probably be delicious. However, I thought I could freestyle the recipe and just switch out the flour for the yellow cake mix since my muffins turned out delicious. You know why they were delicious? Because I actually followed a recipe. I paid attention to the details—ingredients, instructions—and the muffins turned out the way they were supposed to. Since I did not follow the directions with the cake, it was not great. Not even a little bit. We could barely get it out of the pan. In fact, I had to scrape it out of the pan. The lesson I learned was that just because I baked something good once didn't mean I was all of a sudden a master baker who could bake without a recipe. The recipe is there for a reason. So is practice. MAGIC is the recipe. Everyday MAGIC is the practice.

The reason we crash and burn at life and at work is because we don't deliberately practice. If you don't deliberately practice, how can you expect to play intentionally? It's just not feasible. If you don't run on a consistent basis but decide to get up and run a marathon tomorrow, your body is literally going to break down. For so many of us, this is how we're tackling our lives and the result is burnout and sometimes even worse.

The other reason we crash and burn is because we don't intentionally rest. You know who rests? People who practice regularly and then play the game giving it all they've got. They know that you need to rest to be able to show up for practice. If you don't go in with the intent of giving your best at practice and when you play, then the idea of resting certainly escapes you.

How you do one thing is how you do everything. You know when you're not giving it your all. When you're half-assing and hoping no one notices. You know when you're looking for credit instead of doing something on purpose for the right reasons. And the people around you—the people who love you—are really smart. They notice when you're doing that too.

The reason why "Practice how you play" is so important to me is because it reflects how I once was. I was living my life in the most performative way possible. I used to justify resting because I worked and did a lot. And even though I did a lot, it was nothing to write home about. Everything I did was fine. But everyday MAGIC isn't about showing up day to day to be "just fine." It's about doing what matters like you actually give a damn. When I look back on it now, I'm like, "Wow, if I knew then what I know now." Before, I would only show up to play for credit—outside approval, social media likes, praise from friends and extended family. However, I would never show up to practice—doing the internal work no one saw, willingly contributing to the team even if I didn't receive praise, or simply trying again even if I didn't get it right the first time.

That's the whole point of practice: to apply an action or process (in this case, MAGIC) consistently so it becomes polished, permanent, and purposeful.

I thought I was entitled to things being easy because I did what I was supposed to. I went to church, I got married and had kids, I had a good job, and I was a nice person. So what? That didn't make me or anyone else immune to doing the work. Those were things that I was fortunate enough to be blessed with because of my circumstances, but I still needed to do the work to maintain those things and, more importantly, to make them matter.

Be clear, everyday MAGIC is not a substitute for doing the work. There is no substitute for doing the work. Everyday MAGIC simply gives you purpose for doing the work.

Truthfully, it's not deep. Just deliberate.

We're benching ourselves without even giving ourselves a chance to get good. If you don't show up to practice, you will not show up when it's time to play the game. Whether the game is motherhood, entrepreneurship, or marriage—there's nothing magical about the spotlight, the stage, the game, or even a perfectly timed moment. You will not magically arrive and become the ultimate version of yourself in those moments. The MAGIC is you doing the work. It's coming in early, leaving late. It's prioritizing your family, getting your home in order, and consistently going to bed on time so you get enough rest.

It's about you doing the work no one sees. It's about practicing more than once in a while. It's about doing the work daily. It's not about the destination; it was always about the journey. It was never just about a magic moment. It was always about everyday MAGIC.

There are three types of people:

Makers
Masters
Magicians

The makers are the kind of people who make a big deal out of doing a little bit of work for praise and credit. They make it to the game, usually late, and go out of their way to make sure all the attention is on them. They believe that their worth is attached to being seen when they perform. Hence, they are performative. They make appearances instead of differences. They fall for the lie that if no one is clapping for them, then what they do doesn't matter. That's who I once was. Maybe this is where you are now. And that's okay. There's always room to grow.

Then, there are the masters. These are the kind of people who are perfectionists. They start off with good intentions but then become attached to the idea of something instead of committing to the work of executing. They plan, and then plan again and rework that plan again. Then they stall on making progress on their work (be it personally or professionally) until the plan becomes right. They swear they'll actually act on the plan once it becomes the master plan. And then the plan ends up becoming the master of them. The plan never becomes right because their obsession with the idea of how perfect something could be robs them of the reality of how good it actually is.

And then, there are magicians. They understand that the results they want in life and what matters to them have a purpose. They focus on the process more than the result because the work is more important. They decide quickly what they are working toward and then get to work. They show up for practice early and leave late. They pay attention to details only to make them better, not perfect. When it's time to play, they show up calmly and execute deliberately because of how much they practice. They may get attention for their results, but they don't allow praise to speed them up or criticism to slow them down. They simply show up again, every day, and do the necessary work. A magician doesn't show up and say, "Watch me practice"; they simply show up, practice, and get results. They show up on purpose.

Whether you're a maker or a master, you're reading this book to become a magician. Someone who understands that they're more than enough, so they do the necessary work every day because it matters to them. I want you to avoid the cancer of mediocrity and commit to a culture of MAGIC in your everyday life.

Most of us lead busy but undisciplined lives. We're confused as to why we don't have the results we want because we have so much random action in our day-to-day. But aimless action will always produce lackluster results, or even worse, a lack of results period.

Like I said, I used to be a maker. Now, I'm a magician. It didn't happen overnight. Remember those LEGO pieces we talked about at the beginning of this book? I had to stop looking for credit for having pieces and remember my purpose of being complete. That required me to understand that my pieces are meaningful to my purpose, that they're aesthetically pleasing in His eyes, and goal-oriented on whatever life task is at hand in an intentional and consistent way. My pieces matter only with that understanding. My pieces come to life with everyday MAGIC. Every time I had a realization that I was more than enough without being everything to everybody, the truth revealed itself to me more and more. Every time I said no and rested instead of pleasing others. Every time I asked for and hired help. Every time I set boundaries and aimed for balance. My everyday MAGIC was unveiled to me in the most honest and beautiful way.

It wasn't too late for me and it's not too late for you. It's not about naturally being a certain way. You don't have to be naturally good at certain things to get certain results. You just have to deliberately show up every day. Everyday MAGIC will meet you where you're at.

Show up to make dinner, like you show up to do a good job at work.

Show up for self-care like you do your marriage.

Delegate like you set boundaries.

Batch like you close all the tabs in your head.

Do all this willingly, intentionally; and then do it again the next day to make it count, make it better, and make it last. Not just on the days you feel like it, but every day so it counts.

Funny enough, the idea of everyday MAGIC was something I came up with years ago for a brand, but they never responded to the idea. I kept it in my heart and prayed that the idea would come to life, thinking that God would open that brand's eyes and they would see how great of a concept it was. Years later, God was like, "Let Me sprinkle a little extra blessing on this and make it even better for her." Everyday MAGIC is no longer merely a content idea for a brand I wanted to work with, it's the framework of my life. And it can be the framework for yours.

God has absolutely blown my mind away with how He blesses me through my everyday MAGIC. When are you going to let Him blow your mind?

It has been one of the greatest honors of my life to write this book for you.

My prayer for you is that you realize how MAGIC you are in His eyes and you see yourself in that same way every day. That you understand when He created you it was wildly meaningful. You are so marvelous and aesthetically pleasing to His eyes. His goal to make you complete was accomplished. He was overwhelmingly intentional when He created you, which is why He is consistent in pouring blessings into your life whenever you make space for Him in it.

I pray that you never dilute yourself by trying to be everything to everyone and remember to give everything you're assigned to do your all. When you wake up in the morning and when you lay your head down at night, I pray that with every fiber of your being you know that you're more than enough, because that is the truth.

I pray you find self-acceptance and discover self-awareness that leads you to deep self-love.

I pray that you make space for yourself to grow, to learn, to change, and to flourish into exactly who you want to be. I pray that you always remember that the most meaningful, aesthetically pleasing, goal-oriented, intentional, and consistent part of everyday showing up is simply committing to doing the work to be your true self.

ACKNOWLEDGMENTS

The fact that I wrote a book blows my mind. It has been a lifelong dream to do so, and the fact that I'm writing acknowledgments overwhelms me.

I thank God for this assignment, this opportunity, and the gift of writing *Everyday MAGIC*. It is easily the most challenging thing I've ever done professionally and the fact that I got it done is because of His grace. Thank you, Lord.

I have to thank myself for pushing through this journey and finishing the job. I'm really proud of myself. REALLY. While being a mom of three, a wife, a CEO, and during a basement renovation and a pandemic, I did the hardest thing I've ever done as a content creator. I gave myself permission not to write a perfect book, but one that matters. Not only did I have to trust God during this process, but I had to trust myself. Creating in confidence is something that I had to do at times even when the confidence was pretend (hey, fake it 'til you make it—LOL!), and I got the job done. I committed to myself to do something big and do it well. Bravo, me.

To Lisa Jackson, my literary agent whose first email to me was the title of this book, thank you, for always rooting for me and encouraging me to go for it. Our conversations and brainstorm sessions really gave me the push I needed at times. You always have my back and I do not take that lightly. I'm beyond grateful for you and the journey this has been.

To Beth Adams, my editor, thank you, for shaping me into an author. I definitely wrote the first draft like a blogger (ha!) and you gently guided me into the right direction. I fell into your lap after some changes, but it absolutely feels like we were always meant to be from the beginning. Your insight has been valuable to me and I am thankful for your patience with me.

To Dr. Jo, my therapist: a million thanks. The work we've done over the last six years put me in the position and mindset to write this book and believe that I'm worthy of doing so. Your feedback and guidance is deeply appreciated.

To Krissy Davis, my right-hand woman for the last eight years, and likely the first person to pre-order the book on Amazon, I am so grateful for you for so many reasons. Your loyalty, commitment, work ethic, and ability to get better are just a few of them, but more because of your heart and friendship. You've been there when I only made a few hundred dollars a month as a blogger and still worked a 9-to-5. Before I was a mom. Before people knew who I was. You've always believed in me, and I'm wildly grateful to you for that. It brings tears to my eyes. That belief kept me going on days I didn't have faith in myself. Thank you, for always being there for me.

To Shaquinta Milton, who always holds me down, thank you, for all your hard work. I appreciate it more than you'll ever know. TMJC is better because you're a part of it. You truly blow me away with your thoughtfulness, work ethic, and willingness to get better. Knowing that I can always rely on and trust you makes my every day better. You're always two steps ahead and you go out of your way to make my days and the work easier. I thank God for you.

To Erica Simmons, my best friend and photographer, you are everything. Your heart is made out of pure gold and your support is priceless. You constantly checked on me, cheered for me, and every time you told me you were proud of me, I was just floored. You never miss as a friend, never, and to say I'm thankful for you is an understatement. Thank you, for always thinking of me, holding me accountable, and encouraging me in the most authentic way. Your friendship is one of my most prized possessions in life.

To my village: Mannie and Denise James, Lance and Teisha James, Ireal James, Tony and Ashley Jackson, Torrence and Erica Simmons, Sean and Michelle Clark (and all of our kids!)—you give me so much joy and purpose. Getting to live my life with you all in it makes it that much better. You guys have shown up for me in both big and small ways and it means so much to me. I love you all so much. I pray thousandfold favor over each of your families.

To my followers, both old and new, whether you have been following me since Mattieologie or you just discovered me because of this book, I'm thankful for you. I appreciate every single encouraging comment and like, and you taking out the time to consume what I've created.

To Momma and Daddy James: I hit the jackpot with the two of

you. Thank you for loving me as your daughter and always encouraging me while being there whenever I need you. I love you.

To Mom and Dad: Being your daughter is one of the greatest honors of my life and I hope I've made you proud. I love you both so much. You guys both came to another country with almost nothing and created a life where you gave me everything. You are my biggest inspirations. It is because of your example that I even knew to go after the kind of life I wanted. You two are *Everyday MAGIC* personified. Thank you for instilling greatness in me and teaching me that I can have anything I want as long as I'm willing to work for it. Thank you for every single thing you've ever done for me.

To Maya, my sister: Your encouragement is one of the biggest blessings in my life. Your confidence in me has always given me permission to go after my dreams—personally and professionally—and I thank you for that. It's a great honor to be your sister, but wow, what a deep privilege it is to be your friend. I love you. I'm grateful for your honesty, authenticity, and kindness. I appreciate your support during this process so much.

To my babies—Maizah Rose, Caliana Lily, and Christian Melokhule—I love the three of you all so much it makes my head spin when I think about it. Thank you for bringing MAGIC, joy, and purpose into my life every day. Making you proud means so much to me, because you inspire me to go after my dreams. I pray that I make you proud and that the way I live my life gives you permission to go after your wildest dreams. Mommy loves you more than you'll ever know.

Christopher, they say save the best for last and that is exactly what you are: THE BEST. I love you deeply. You are my rock. I have never

ABOUT THE AUTHOR

Mattie James is a full-time content creator, lifestyle influencer, and CEO of The Mattie James Company. She creates lifestyle content for her blog, mattiejames.com, Instagram, and YouTube channel while working with brands like Samsung, T.J.Maxx, and J.Crew. After being crowned Miss Liberia USA in 2009, Mattie started her blog as a hobby and grew it into the seven-figure business it is today. She's taught thousands of content creators and influencers how to grow their following, pitch brands, and create content for profit with her online courses and programs. She currently lives in Atlanta with her husband and three beautiful children.